GUARDED BY ANGELS
Memoir of a Dutch youth in WWII

Alard. B Ages

Al Ages

29 juni '07

To Sobat Juul, our Great Dane
who didn't make it.
1938 - 1943

Note for Librarians: A cataloguing record for this book is available from Library and Archives Canada at www.collectionscanada.ca/amicus/index-e.html
ISBN 1-4251-1804-6

Printed in Victoria, BC, Canada. Printed on paper with minimum 30% recycled fibre. Trafford's print shop runs on "green energy" from solar, wind and other environmentally-friendly power sources.

Offices in Canada, USA, Ireland and UK

Book sales for North America and international:
Trafford Publishing, 6E–2333 Government St.,
Victoria, BC V8T 4P4 CANADA
phone 250 383 6864 (toll-free 1 888 232 4444)
fax 250 383 6804; email to orders@trafford.com
Book sales in Europe:
Trafford Publishing (UK) Limited, 9 Park End Street, 2nd Floor
Oxford, UK OX1 1HH UNITED KINGDOM
phone +44 (0)1865 722 113 (local rate 0845 230 9601)
facsimile +44 (0)1865 722 868; info.uk@trafford.com
Order online at:
trafford.com/07-0216

10 9 8 7 6 5 4 3 2

CONTENTS

i

FOREWORD

Some years ago, when I visited schools in the province of British Columbia to lecture about the effect of oil spills on the marine environment, I once addressed a graduating class (grade 12) in the northern community of Fort St. John, just after the Canadian television network had shown an impressive documentary of the liberation of Holland by the Canadians in 1945. Upon my arrival, the principal told me that he had heard from one of his colleagues elsewhere that I had attended a Dutch high school (gymnasium, Leiden) during the German occupation, and he suggested that I switch my topic from "oil spills" to "life at a Dutch school during the German occupation in the early forties." Many of his students had been watching the documentary with great interest. Having no slides or films on this rather novel topic, I reluctantly agreed and was given some time to refresh my memory.

I told the packed audience of seventeen- and eighteen-year-old boys and girls about a girl in our class being ostracized by everybody throughout our years at school because one of her parents was German; of the girl in front of me, who disappeared one day, presumably because she was Jewish and had been sent to a concentration camp; and of our very respected and popular math teacher, who was taken hostage by the Nazis and executed. I described how occasionally some of us boys had to go into hiding because we had done something patriotic, while the girls during our absence copied the lecture notes every night without, of course, having the convenience of a photocopier. Throughout all this, there were the almost daily overflights of not hundreds but thousands of British and American bombers en route to the industrial cities of Germany. One of the teachers who listened from the back row told me at the conclusion of my talk that her class had never been so quiet and suggested that I put these stories into writing some day. So here is *Guarded by Angels: Memoir of a Dutch Youth in WWII.*

Netherlands

0 10 20 30 kilometers
0   10   20   30 miles

NORTH
SEA

Groningen

Grouw

Sneek

Afsluit
Dijk

IJsselmeer

Haarlem
Amsterdam

Leiden
Wassenaar
The
Hague
Utrecht

Arnhem

Rotterdam
Sliedrecht
Dordrecht

Tilburg

Eindhoven

Antwerp

GERMANY

BELGIUM

1

THE ONSLAUGHT, 10TH MAY, 1940

They came just before day break, almost peacefully and still hidden by the darkness of the pre-dawn sky. Living only a few kilometres from a large military airport, we were used to the sound of aircraft engines and at first paid little attention to the noise overhead.

Startled by the unmistakable sound of a nearby anti-aircraft battery at day break, I leaned out of my bedroom window in the attic and noticed several large planes milling around above the village. According to my little manual on the identification of war planes, they were Junkers 52 transports and their Luftwaffe markings became now quite visible. My father ran up the stairs to join me at the window, complaining that our air force should find some other location for their training flights.

"Papa," I said, "get with it. Look at their markings. They are not ours." I was fifteen years old.

Papa trained his fancy Zeiss binoculars on the planes and stammered, "Wel God verdomme, de Moffen!" Then he scanned the fields north of our street and spotted hundreds of little dots descending from the Junkers.

"Parachutisten." He grumbled, "I told Rassers that they'd attack here in the west, not from the German border, but nobody listened."

Professor Rassers, director of the archeological museum in Leiden, and my father, an engineer, commuted daily at the same time and amused other commuters with their political and strategic views.

Most people were well aware of the possibility of a German invasion after Hitler had annexed Austria, had manipulated the breakup
of Czecho Slovakia, then overran Poland and Denmark and attacked
Norway. Preceding the outbreak of the war between England and
France versus Germany, the Dutch mobilized in August, 1939 and
were well prepared. However, few of us expected our peaceful
coastal town to be almost immediately on the frontline when much
of the country was still asleep.

Wassenaar, with close to thirty thousand inhabitants, is situated
just north of The Hague, the seat of the Dutch government and the
residence of the Queen. The village centre, with its main street
and large Catholic church, borders on an extensive area of estates
and villas owned by the affluent, and on a much smaller district
occupied by the less affluent, mostly professionals such as my parents. There are still vast open fields to the north, and several rows
of dunes protect the area against the storm waves of the North Sea
during the winter.

My mother walked in crying. She had turned on the radio to hear
announced a declaration of war with Germany. She worried about
Frits, my oldest brother, who was a mate in the Nederland Line and,
after a year at sea in the Far East, would finally be on his way home.
But Frits was also in the Dutch Naval Reserve as commandant of a
torpedo boat and would almost certainly be called up by our Navy
as soon as he'd arrived home. We tried to console mother that he
would be better off staying at sea away from Holland than going
down with his torpedo boat or being taken prisoner. Little did we
foresee he would be away until the end of the war five years later,
having survived torpedoes and bombs in the Atlantic and Pacific.
My other brother Nap, a journalist, lived in The Hague.

While we were discussing brother Frits, a peleton of fifty elite
huzaren (motorized hussars) passed below our window on their
Harley Davidsons to meet the advancing German paratroopers.
These Dutch soldiers were encamped in the primary school down
the road and had made many local friends. As we learned the next
day, only six survived the encounter with the Germans.

I went outside to calm our animals, the bantam chickens in their run, two nervous cats hiding under the fence and, most of all, our Great Dane, Sobat (Malayan for "friend"), who had joined virtually every dog in the neighbourhood in their continuous barking and howling at the commotion up above. As I stepped out in our yard, a large bloodied bird literally fell out of the sky right in front of me: a dead falcon, most likely having strayed into the shrapnel of exploding anti-aircraft grenades. I wrapped it in a towel and buried it under our birch tree, but the sight of this lifeless magnificent bird somehow kept haunting me, more than that of the carnage around us in the following days.

We occasionally ventured onto the roof and noticed tiny pieces of molten metal flattened on impact, obviously shrapnel. We spotted only two Dutch aircraft in the air that morning. They were totally outnumbered and outclassed by the Messerschmidts and Heinkels. A Dutch Fokker T5 light bomber showed up, firing from a turret in its tail, and disappeared behind the dunes; then there was a small outdated Fokker D21 fighter (canvas over aluminum frame) harassing the German paratroopers until it was hit by German fighters and skimmed belly up between the paratroopers in the field. We learned later that the pilot, unhurt, played dead upside down in the cockpit for several hours, ignored by the Germans. He survived and was freed from the plane by the Dutch when the Germans were forced back. A couple of days after the end of the hostilities, I reached the wreck with my friend Willem Thijsse in our kayaks and cannibalized an acrylic window to cut rings out for the girls at school to put on their fingers. I presented the first such work of art to my mother.

The Germans appeared to temporarily secure the airport at Valkenburg, five kilometres north of Wassenaar, later in the morning and started to land ground troops to back up the paratroopers, who seemed to become less effective without the initial element of surprise. The Junkers carrying these troops had to approach the airport at a very low altitude, barely clearing trees and houses. Their flight path passed over a nearby bridge where our soldiers had set up a well-hidden site to shoot at the transports but, lacking an AA gun, they used their rifles. It didn't take our local youth very long to learn about this interesting activity and we soon joined the soldiers in taking potshots at the bellies and cockpits of the lumbering aircraft whenever we got hold of some unattended rifles. I might add here that very few families in Holland have any interest in using firearms to go hunting or target shooting so, to us teenagers in civilized Wassenaar, it was quite an experience to try a shot at a Junkers with a real rifle. At a nearby site (Maaldrift), the cockpit of a low-flying Junkers was hit; the Ju52 started to wobble, dove into the ground and exploded in flames. The rifle shot might have hit the pilot.

The German pilots still had to face the Dutch artillery hidden behind hangars at the airport of Valkenburg and the coastal guns that had been turned around to target the landing Junkers. About five minutes after a plane had passed over us, we noticed a column of black smoke rise above the airport followed by the distant rumble of our heavy coastal artillery somewhere in the dunes.

I went home to have a snack and visit our scared animals. However, when I left again to return to the bridge, my father stopped me and told me to stay away from that "shooting gallery" in case a Stuka (German dive-bombers; Stuka stands for Sturzkampf Flugzeug) would be called in to drop a bomb and eliminate all of us on the bridge. I noticed he was wearing an air defence arm band and had become one of the local officials, so I didn't argue with him. Similar discussions had obviously occurred in other households because none of my buddies returned to the site. Moreover, the transports didn't either.

Later we wondered if and how far a rifle-caliber bullet would travel inside a Junkers after it had penetrated the corrugated light aluminum fuselage as the aircraft approached at a relatively low speed. We would have liked to examine the wrecked planes after the immediate hostilities had ended, but were unable to get by the German guards. My father somehow walked by the guard and counted forty-one disabled Junkers on the runway. He did not examine the insides of the planes. My father occasionally walked past a German guard without identification simply by acting like an authority – well-dressed and speaking fluent German, which he had learned when he represented Dutch ship owners (the Nederland Line) ordering heavy machinery in Germany and Switzerland. He and the guard would strike up a friendly conversation (e.g., about the guard's family or home town) and my father would then just walk on. He actually demonstrated this to me once when we were cycling near a German fortification at Scheveningen, just west of The Hague. He told me to watch him from a distance. He pulled it off nicely, but I told him that he would never get past a Dutch guard and he agreed. Before the German invasion, Queen Wilhelmina inspected a coastal artillery site near Scheveningen and was stopped by the Dutch guard asking for her I.D. She had none and couldn't get in and left. It was in all our newspapers. At any event, one got the impression that the average German soldier felt insecure in Holland and could easily be bluffed as long as there was no officer nearby.

My father and I spent the afternoon and the next day securing the house and our possessions against air attacks and the likelihood of a future German occupation. Mother went shopping for food supplies. My father sadly dumped all our wine, beer and liqueur into the toilet upon the advise of the authorities. He then hid my brother's uniform, parade hat and sword. He never mentioned a revolver, possibly to keep it out of the reach of junior (me). We secured the glass in all the windows with paper strips to protect us from falling glass, and we stored some paintings. We then stored hundreds of Delfia margarine bricks (which had arrived after mother's expedition to the grocery store) in between the beams supporting the first floor. Here we made a bad mistake. During a hot day a few weeks later, the fat melted through the paper wrapping, into the plaster, through the ceiling and down into the dining room and living room. My parents stood there in disbelief, watching the drips of fat descending on our furniture, our Persian carpets and my mother's grand piano. The entire ceiling had to be replaced, among other repairs.

My father and I did a better job storing our valuables (shares, certificates, some gold) in a hole which we dug underneath some marked tiles in the garage floor. The valuables were protected against ground water in a glass watertight container.

There was an eerie silence in our street at nightfall of the first day of hostilities. I took our dog out for a walk, followed within a few metres by one of our cats. Apart from a few soldiers on patrol, the street was deserted and the street lights were off. Most of the houses were dark and locked as a precaution against prowling paratroopers. I could hear some bursts of machine gun fire in the nearby fields, but it didn't seem to bother the animals any more. Our tomcat Pier (from *rode piraat*, Dutch for red pirate) liked to go for walks with us, feeling safe with big Sobat to protect him from other dogs. They were great friends and it was a real treat in the turmoil around us to watch Sobat and Pier peacefully sleep in the same large basket with Pier curled up between the fore paws of the huge and gentle Great Dane.

2

A NATION CONFUSED

After the first tumultuous day, the assault of the German paratroopers in the fields between Wassenaar and Valkenburg seemed to degenerate into sporadic skirmishes in the dunes and the outskirts of Wassenaarr. In the evening of May 12th, we were jolted by machine gun fire from the belfry of a nearby church with an almost immediate response by rifle fire from our soldiers in the surrounding gardens and balconies, until a few blasts from an anti-tank gun in the adjoining street shattered the belfry and part of the tower. We didn't know whether the killed snipers were Fallschirmjäger, or Dutch Nazis, and didn't bother to find out.

There had been persistent reports of a significant fifth column of members of the Dutch Nazi party (NSB) and Germans living in the Netherlands, sniping from buildings and providing paratroopers with pre-arranged transportation. (The term "fifth column" dates back to the Spanish Civil War, when four columns of Franco's fascists approached Madrid in 1936, supported by a "fifth column" which had earlier infiltrated the city.)

Because of the threat of German paratroopers or Dutch Nazis shooting from houses, we had to keep our windows closed and some of our more cautious neighbours had barricaded their doors. An eight-to-ten curfew was enforced by patrols of soldiers assisted by local armed volunteers. Everybody had to carry identification and street cars passing through our street were regularly searched.

Many arrests were made even before the outbreak of hostilities, when a prominent member of the Lower House in The Hague (Mr. Rost van Tonningen) was interned. Almost immediately after the landing of the German paratroops, two nearby houses were searched by the police, alerted by an old lady next door. They found a shortwave transmitter and carried out a truckload of documents. The occupants were arrested and we never saw them again.

While occupied with the events in our own part of the country, we hardly followed the rapid developments elsewhere. There were no newspapers; TV, of course, did not yet exist. The radio was our sole source of information and we were cautioned to trust only the familiar voices of the three regular ANP announcers in case a radio station had been taken over by Dutch Nazis. Somehow it took three days until we became aware of the devastating news that the strategic Moerdijk bridges had been captured by German paratroops almost immediately during the first day of the war.

Obviously dismissing the threat of an airdrop, the defence of the Moerdijk bridges had delayed a state of alarm by one day after the enemy had crossed the eastern border. The explosives under the bridges had yet to be installed when the paratroopers descended on the bridgeheads and captured the bridges intact.

The Dutch preparedness against a German invasion had focused on the defence of Fort Holland, covering the western provinces of North and South Holland and Utrecht, directly accessible over land from the north via the Afsluitdijk (a barrier dam built in earlier years to close off and reclaim the Zuiderzee); from the south via the large Moerdijk bridges; and protected from the east by fortresses (the Grebbe Line) and inundated land to disable the German heavy armour. Gun emplacements along the Dutch coast provided evidence of our intended neutrality in case of a conflict between our mighty neighbours. However, the German invasion forced the Netherlands as well as Belgium to request military assistance from Britain and France, which was immediately granted.

Much to the relief of my father and his expert political cronies, on May 11th Neville Chamberlain was replaced as Prime Minister of Great Britain by the old warrior Winston Churchill. Churchill welcomed the "indomitable" Dutch over the BBC with his usual flowery rhetoric. Unfortunately, with the loss of the Moerdijk bridges, the indomitable Dutch had just squandered one of their most dependable defences against the German advance. Other setbacks were our failure to recapture the large airport of Waalhaven, Rotterdam, and the collapse of the Grebbe Line.

Contrary to our high expectations, the promised and desperately needed French and British military aid consisted only of a small contingent of French troops briefly crossing into our southern provinces while the R.A.F. raided Waalhaven. The French withdrew before being dragged along by retreating Dutch forces and refugees. There were reports that British marines landed in IJmuiden and had to be dissuaded from blowing up the locks at the entrance of the canal leading to the port of Amsterdam. Without these locks, parts of the province of North Holland would be flooded. Moreover, one of our older passenger ships, the *Jan Pieterszoon Coen* of the Nederland Line, was scuttled in the entrance, blocking any marine traffic to Amsterdam throughout the German occupation.

Apart from an occasional *acte de présence* of a couple of Spitfires over our village, we noticed little of the much heralded British support of our badly outclassed air force of 118 battle-ready planes. Of course, we were hardly aware of the precarious position in which our allies were about to find themselves, leaving them with no other option than to protect their own retreating troops.

All Dutch aircraft were eventually destroyed, but not before they had had their share in the destruction of close to 500 German planes over Holland. Many of our state-of-the-art Fokker G1 fighter-bombers, with their then-unique double tails, were destroyed by the Luftwaffe before they even left the tarmac. While strafing or bombing the German ground troops in our fields, pilots of some very old Dutch aircraft were seen to avoid a dogfight with a much faster Messerschmidt by flying near ground level, forcing the enemy to overshoot the Dutch plane, which would then regain altitude and continue its strafing.

To preserve the posterity of the House of Orange, Princess Juliana and her two daughters, Beatrix and Irene, left the palace in The Hague and boarded a British destroyer in Ijmuiden to be taken safely to England. Her husband, Prince Bernhard, stayed behind as an *aide de champs* of the Queen. The next day, Queen

Wilhelmina was urged by the Commander-in-Chief of the Dutch forces, General Winkelman, to immediately leave Holland, as the German tanks were already near Rotterdam, about twenty kilometres from The Hague. She reluctantly left on a British destroyer off Hoek van Holland, later followed by members of the Cabinet. Over a thousand captured German pilots and specialists were also transferred to England as well as part or all of the gold reserves.

The Queen eventually ended up in Buckingham Palace, from where she immediately delivered a proclamation to explain the reasons behind her departure and that of her ministers. In it, there was not a word of compassion for the soldiers fallen while preventing her capture by the German paratroopers during their failed attempt to conquer The Hague and the palace. As a young princess and the only heir to the throne some hundred years ago today, she had been groomed relentlessly for her future position and had developed into a proud and tough lady not known for compassion. Her pride was exactly why we had not expected her to leave the country and we wondered how her Commander-in-Chief convinced her to do so. The departure of the Queen and her cabinet (the "flight," as Nazi propaganda called it) did not demoralize us as expected by the Nazis. We were shaken more by the military fiascos in the south and east of the country, the wild and often false rumours of betrayal, and the stench of corpses of men and animals in the local fields and dunes.

During the afternoon of May 14th, black columns started to appear on the southern horizon. They kept growing throughout the afternoon until they became a huge black cloud covering part of the horizon, changing into a red glow after sunset. We turned on the radio; Rotterdam was burning. The Germans had bombed the city and informed our Commander-in-Chief that the city of Utrecht would be next if the Dutch did not capitulate. General Winkelman wisely ordered his forces to lay down their arms.

The lights in the street went back on that night. Then there were again rifle shots. They were from frustrated soldiers trying to shoot the lights out.

When the radio announced the capitulation, the citizens as well as the soldiers in Wassenaar were shocked and incredulous, in particular since the military and the local administration in our area seemed to have stabilized the commotion of the first three days. Having so far survived a violent and ruthless campaign around The Hague, few of us were prepared to give up that quickly, certainly not our soldiers, who had lost so many of their comrades in a few days. We may not extend this comment to a nationwide reaction because of the way other provinces had been affected by the invasion. Of the two most densely populated and industrial provinces constituting Holland, the southern province, Zuid Holland, immediately became the scene of bitter fighting around The Hague and Rotterdam. However, the northern half, Noord Holland, with the Netherlands' capital Amsterdam, remained virtually untouched, as did Friesland and Groningen in the north east.

Whatever the reaction to our military surrender might have been, there would be no difference of opinion or pardon anywhere in the country with respect to the Dutch Nazis and their sympathizers.

3

UNEXPECTED HOUSE GUESTS

The first German panzers arrived quietly in The Hague and Wassenaar in the morning of the 15th of May. The tank crews did not wave and neither did the subdued spectators. All imprisoned Dutch Nazis had been released promptly after the capitulation the night before, but most of them had the good sense to stay out of sight. Trains started to run again and in The Hague, large crowds were boarding trains to Rotterdam to learn about the fate of relatives and friends. Compared to the destruction of part of Rotterdam, The Hague and environs in the line of fire during the paratroop assault had sustained only minor damage. Apart from a couple of shattered tiles and a broken window possibly caused by the shooting from the church tower, our own house had remained unscathed.

In retrospect, the wanton destruction of part of Rotterdam by the Luftwaffe and the threat of a similar fate to other open cities made any further resistance absurd, in particular since our government had slipped out of the country. But why was Rotterdam selected as the first target? Were the German technocrats perhaps thinking of preparing the renovation of this city into a more efficient transit centre in the waterway to West Germany?

Immediately after the capitulation, our neighbourhood received word from the municipal hall to billet German paratroopers who had survived the battle around Wassenaar and Valkenburg. The residents could only guess at the origins of this insensitive order, but complied in view of the explosive atmosphere all around. My parents were asked to host two paratroopers and, to my surprise, they seemed to comply more out of curiosity than out of fear for reprisal.

Our house guests arrived May 17th, three days after the capitulation. I opened the door and faced two paratroopers in full uniform. Both saluted smartly.

"Wir sind der Franz und der Ensinger."

I froze and ran to the kitchen to whisper to my mother that the Germans were at the door. Mother did not seem the least bit shaken and went to meet them.

"Kommen Sie herein bitte."

She let them in the living room, made some tea and asked them about their home and family, just like my father would do. They looked very young, not much older than my fifteen years. They told her that they were from Bayern and Schlezien. I suddenly realized that my mother spoke fluent German like my father and actually much better than myself after my four years at the gymnasium (an institution in between high school and college in North America) where we were taught more grammar than conversation.

One of the first things we noticed about these two men was their almost impeccable behaviour, at the dinner table and around the house. Conversations with my parents were wide open. They did not attempt to indoctrinate us about Naziism and evidently had not been instructed to do so. My parents gave them a piece of their mind on this topic and they listened, probably because they realized that both my parents were familiar with their country and their regime. That wasn't always the case in the other households where paratroopers were billeted. Although my German was not good enough to participate in those dialogues, I could understand their conversations quite well and I admired my parents for the way they handled themselves, politically as well as linguistically. After all, they could have been reported by our guests as *deutsch feindlich* (anti-German), but they didn't care. The two troopers in vain tried to convince us that they were sent out to protect our country against a planned English invasion (*lächerlich*, my father called it: ludicrous) and that they were surprised that they had to fight the Dutch instead. They had been prepared and politically indoctrinated for their "mission" in isolation for several weeks.

Our daily conversations with our two house guests left us with the clear impression that the almost flawlessly prepared surprise attack by the Germans on The Hague and surrounding airports had failed, at a tremendous cost of men and equipment. They confirmed my father's count of forty wrecked Junkers transporters on the airport at Valkenburg and told us their version in detail. A Dutch anti-tank gun had been set up behind a hangar and when a Junkers carrying ground troops landed, the gun shelled the plane's nose and centre engine (the Ju 52 has three engines) as soon as it passed its field of fire. According to the troopers, when one plane after another had been disabled, the remaining Junkers, with the ground troops still on board, aborted the landing to return to Germany. Some of them landed on the beach near Wassenaar and sank so far into the sand that they could not fly out again. Of their company of one hundred and forty paratroopers, only forty had survived the battle in the fields near Wassenaar, and their colleagues in the other companies did not fare much better. They seemed to have been more worried about crawling around in our muddy fields and spending night after night in a watery ditch than being shot out of the air by Dutch snipers during their descent with a parachute.

Despite our guests' sincere and unassuming conduct, we still had to struggle with the knowledge that these two guys were professional killers who might well have shot some Dutch hussars passing our house on their motorbikes during that fatal Friday morning. For me, the visit of the two German paratroopers had been a significant learning experience. As a somewhat cocky teenager, I had considered my parents as a nice couple with limited education and a lack of interest in anything outside their own milieu. Their style in dealing with a difficult situation surprised me and made me feel, well, like a teenager.

Der Franz and der Ensinger departed on May 27th, ten days after their arrival. They were joined by the other survivors who had been billeted in our neighbourhood. They collectively presented the boys in the neighbourhood with a brand new Harley Davidson motorcycle with side car, probably captured from the Dutch army. It went to the only one among us who was eighteen and had a driver's license. We had several joyrides in the neighbourhood until the local police confiscated it. We suspected that the worried father of the new owner alerted the police.

Six years later, I arrived in the then-Dutch East Indies as an apprentice on the ship the *Tarakan,* carrying relief goods as well as supplies and war materials for the Dutch marines who had landed earlier to re-occupy Java after the Japanese surrendered. Part of our cargo consisted of one hundred caterpillar-tracked Bren gun carriers. After one of the marines had shown us how to manipulate these weird, noisy vehicles, we navigated them around in the cargo hold to be winched to the dock where they were handed over to the marines. Being rushed and inexperienced, my colleague apprentice Jaap Kelderman and I sometimes drove our carriers right over other cargo stored in the same hold, crushing and mixing boxes of condensed milk and the face-blackening powder used for night operations, making our faces unrecognizable and the butt of much merriment among the marines waiting on the dock.

Several of these men may well have been the same legendary warriors who had distinguished themselves during the battle around Rotterdam in May of 1940. The Germans respectfully called them *die Schwarzen* (the black ones) because of their black uniforms. We didn't recognize them as such. They looked more like members of Rommel's Afrika Corps or Montgomery's Desert Rats: shirtless, tanned, with sunglasses, shorts and a sporty little hat. As Jaap K. and I watched the last vehicle leave the dock, my thoughts went back to the German paratroopers who swooped down on our fields during that peaceful morning in May of 1940 and I wondered if our mariniers (Dutch marines) or the German Fallschirmjäger really knew what they were in for when they signed up for either type of military elite.

The mariniers have often been mentioned in our Dutch military folklore and again they didn't disappoint. There were many stories about their hand-to-hand combat with the German paratroopers on and below the bridges leading to Rotterdam, and with German commandos who came ashore with inflatables released from Dornier seaplanes landing on the river near the city.

4

FAMILY AND FRIENDS

My father, Jelte Ages, was born in 1873 in De Lemmer, the main access of Friesland to the Zuiderzee in the 19th century. Friesland, now named Fryslân, is the northernmost province of the Netherlands and still has its own language, although Dutch is also taught at school. Jelte's father was captain and owner of a large sailing vessel that was based in De Lemmer and carried freight to and from the Baltic. According to Jelte, his father lost his trade when he stubbornly refused to convert his ship to steam power. He succumbed to alcohol, a frustrated and angry man. After his death, Jelte set up a boarding house in The Hague to be run by his sister Tante Rens (tante means "aunt"), and their widowed mother, whom we called Opemoeke (Frisian for "grandma"). The baby brother of Jelte and Rens tragically died of croup.

Descending from a captain for a father and a De Lemmer harbour master for a grandfather, Jelte was naturally familiar with a sea farer's life. However, he did not quite tread in his father's footsteps, but attended an engineer's school to become a ship's engineer with the Nederland Line in Amsterdam in around 1900. After several years at sea, he went on to become director of a ship yard near Rotterdam and subsequently returned to the Nederland Line to supervise engine design for large passenger vessels.

Born in Amsterdam in 1893, my mother, Aleida Regina van Weel, was brought up in the somewhat Bohemian district of that city. My mother never mentioned her real father to us, her children. I think he was some artist who came and vanished, leaving a daughter with considerable artistic talent. She once hinted to us that she had a brother and my father confirmed it but added that he was a good-for-nothing and had to be thrown out of the house when he called to borrow money from his sister. He never came back.

My mother lived with her mother throughout her youth and while she studied music at the Conservatory. After graduating, she played violin with the Concertgebouw Orkest in Amsterdam under Mengelberg. She did not like him because he had green eyes and he spent a long time reading his fan letters at the start of a rehearsal, keeping the orchestra waiting. During the German occupation, Mengelberg made no secret of his support of the Nazis. He must have liked Wagner.

My mother's studies at the Conservatory had apparently been financed by a platonic friend of her mother, a very nice gentleman whom we called Opa, Dutch for "grandfather," and who was like a father to my mother. Opa's real name was Frits Suidema. Like my father, he was a ship's engineer with the Nederland Line but unlike my father, who eventually left the company to take a position in a shipyard, Opa remained at sea. He was a chief engineer when he retired and married a lady in Amsterdam whom we got to know as Tante Miel.

The two engineers seldom served on the same ship, but they happened to be shipmates on New Year's Day in 1900 on the Prins van Oranje when the vessel broke her propeller shaft in the Indian Ocean, leaving her drifting helplessly with no land in sight and no ships in the vicinity. My father, an experienced sailor, suggested the captain send out a sloop to make for Sumatra and find help, perhaps locate a tugboat to tow their ship to the port of Padang where they might wait for a new shaft. The captain went along with the idea and a small group of seven volunteers – my father, Opa, four seamen and a mate with his sextant, chronometer and nautical almanac – set out eastward to Sumatra. After several days of sailing in open water, their landfall was the island of Nias along the northern part of Sumatra. One might be somewhat puzzled by the sloop's arrival near Nias, about two hundred nautical miles Northwest of Padang, assuming that the position of the *Prins van Oranje* was accurately established by celestial observations and that the sloop was almost certainly heading for Padang.

"Why can't we expect accurate results from celestial observations taken on a small, lively boat while we don't have this problem with GPS?" a modern reader might ask. Before the introduction of GPS, navigation in open water (i.e., no coast in sight) involved measuring the vertical angle of a star with the horizontal. A note on celestial navigation might help the uninitiated reader get an idea of the problem facing navigation in a lively sloop without GPS.

"Shooting stars" involves measuring the vertical angle of a star (or moon or sun) with the horizontal (the actual horizon with a few corrections). All observers who measure the same height (vertical angle) of the same star at the same time are standing on a circle around the projection of this star on the earth's surface. Knowing the celestial coordinates of that star from our almanac and the exact time from a chronometer (at Greenwich, to look up these coordinates), we can construct a small segment of that circle in the form of a straight line. We do the same with two or three other stars and plot a small square or triangle with our position at its centre. The angles must be perfectly vertical and it takes experience to hold a sextant on the swaying deck of a vessel riding the swell. However, it would be foolish to expect a reliable starfix on a rolling and pitching launch. In that respect, GPS has a clear advantage. GPS needs no skill, no understanding. To a dedicated navigator, GPS sadly is somewhat like computerized music to a creative musician. Both transform us into robots, skilled only in pushing the right button.

Unfortunately, a quick check of the latitude by sighting Polaris was impossible because, at the equator, Polaris is on the horizon. At any rate, according to my father, they hesitated to go ashore because of the hostile attitude of the local population towards the Dutch in those days. With supplies running low, they had started to proceed southward along the inhospitable coast when two ships appeared on the horizon. The sloop headed out and, to everyone's relief, one of the silhouettes was soon recognized as that of their own *Prins van Oranje* being towed by another vessel, which proved to be the *Princess Sophie*, also of the Nederland Line. The *Sophie* had found the lost *Prins van Oranje* in distress, took her in tow to

Padang and en route picked up the sloop. It was a happy reunion for the crew. Although the risky endeavour by the seven volunteers had been no factor in the rescue of the Prins van Oranje, they were later honoured with a reception by the shipping company's board of directors in Amsterdam and each presented with a hand-engraved document and a golden watch. One hundred years later, the recent introduction of GPS in our navigation would have made the outcome of this adventure much more predictable, but much less challenging to a navigator.

Aleid van Weel and Jelte Ages were married in Calcutta in 1912. I understand from the little my parents told me that Aleid was en route to the Dutch East Indies (now Indonesia) to help set up a music school in the capital Batavia (now Jakarta), while Jelte happened to be there on business. They had known each other for some time in Amsterdam when Opa and Jelte happened to be in port at the same time and visited Aleid and her mother. Sadly, Aleid's mother, who accompanied her on her voyage to the Far East, died of peritonitis during their stay in Calcutta. Aleid ended her voyage and returned to Holland with Jelte. They settled near Amsterdam. Brothers Frits and Nap were born in 1913 and 1914, followed by me in 1924, shortly after the family had returned from a year with my father in Winterthur, Switzerland, where he was involved with the design of the Sulzer engines for the liner *Johan van Oldebarnevelt*. My two brothers were then ten and eleven years old and went to a Swiss school while my mother looked after the rented house, cooked and took lessons in yodelling and zither. The family became quite fluent in the Swiss version of German spoken in Winterthur.

Upon their return to the Netherlands, my parents rented a small house in the town of Soestdijk near the grounds of the royal palace of Princess Juliana. I never lost an opportunity to point out to my friends that not only was I "made in Switzerland" (a valuable endorsement for any product!), but I had also been Princess Juliana's neighbour. A friend in Holland sent me a recent picture of that family house; nothing had changed in 80 years: the advantage of bricks and tiles made of baked clay.

As regards the *Johan van Oldebarnevelt*, the ship which gradually became so closely associated with my father and his family, the *JvO* became a troopship of the allies during the war. I had the pleasure to serve as a third mate on this magnificent vessel after the war when, as a Nederland Line vessel, she transported thousands of women from Holland and England to the Far East to be reunited with their men.

The *JvO* introduced me to radar as a leftover from her wartime duties. Its scanner was mounted high up on the forward mast and the operator, crammed in a crow's nest just below the scanner, had to turn it manually from within while staring at a small scope with a line of grassy signals caused by water waves. A large green blade on that line could be a vessel. Crossing the Bay of Biscay in dense fog, I was sent up the mast during my watch before day break. With my left hand covering my mouth so as not to be sick and turning the scanner's handle with my right hand, I spotted a large signal which did not go away but instead moved closer to the centre of the scope. I phoned the bridge and the slowly moving *JvO* stopped immediately. Then I heard the other vessel's whistle, she having stopped as well. The two ships slowly moved around each other and went on their way again. Quite an introduction to basic electronic navigation!

I was sad to learn in 1963 that the *Johan van Oldebarnevelt* was sold to Greece, renamed Lakonia, burnt out near Madeira with a loss of one hundred and twenty eight passengers and crew and sank while being towed to Gibraltar. A retired Irish friend in the scientific community at the Institute of Ocean Sciences on Vancouver Island, Dr. Pat Crean, still reminisces fondly about the *JvO*. As a young mechanic, he was doing repairs in the engine room in Liverpool while the docks were bombed by German aircraft. He had some nice things to say about the engine room, which was still equipped with the engines my father helped to design, but unfortunately my father wasn't there to hear them.

While supervising the design of engines for other vessels of the Nederland Line, my father regularly travelled to Germany (M.A.N in Augsburg), England and Italy. My mother, called "Mam" by her children, had her own travel schedule. Over the years, she was the author of eight novels in Dutch and used the proceeds mostly to travel to Austria for a couple of weeks at a time to be part of a musical ensemble and continue her lessons in yodelling and zither. My father then had to look after the household, sometimes with Marijke, a friend of my mother's, or a hired local girl, Stien. This arrangement between our father and mother was far from common in those days, certainly in Holland. Also far from common was the twenty years age difference between our parents, although the traditional and rigid pre-war Dutch society would be disrupted by the German occupation and subsequent liberation by the immensely popular and unpretentious Canadians.

My mother was a rebel. She was one of the first women to cut her hair short and to wear slacks. My father was no stranger to new ideas either and his everlasting *joie de vivre* made their age difference insignificant. Although generally the more demonstrably affectionate parent, once in a while his patriarchal status surfaced at the dinner table during an argument between my mother and my two brothers when I, the baby brother, became upset and started to cry. My father growled a bit at everybody and promptly stopped the arguing. Mam and my father got on very well together and never argued.

Normally we had our dinner *en famille*. Mam cooked and my father washed the dishes. The sessions where lively, everybody talking all the time, mostly about world events. After the dessert, we all withdrew to our own private little worlds. When she worked on one of her novels, my mother even locked her door so as not to be interrupted. My parents always studied: languages, philosophy, music theory, ship's engines. Mam even took Swedish when she was well into her sixties, while my father took Latin and math with me during my first year at the gymnasium.

Apart from cooking dinner, my mother left much of the household to Stien, who came every day except Sunday. In those days, several reasonably well-off families in Holland employed local girls who had finished elementary school and didn't want to continue or could not because of low marks or need for money. Although liked and well treated by all in the family, if Stien stayed for dinner, she had to eat in the kitchen. I don't know why, but that was the way my mother organized things, perhaps simply because Stien wasn't really part of the family. She also had her own little washroom near the kitchen. When I misbehaved during meals, I had to eat with Stien. Being so much younger than any other member of the family and not particularly interested in their table conversation, I didn't consider eating in the kitchen a punishment, especially not when we had turnips or purslane for dinner. Mam never found out what happened to these vegetables in the kitchen and Stien didn't let on. Stien had been with us well over ten years when my parents moved north to Friesland.

Although not a solitary child by nature, before I was eleven years old and started to attend the gymnasium in Leiden, my own private little world in the evening was a large, three-by-three metre shallow pool which, supervised by my father, I had built in our backyard out of concrete and chicken wire. I simulated naval battles with little warships in real water, my interests in all things naval following those of the family. The combatant fleets were Spanish, English and Dutch, as dinner conversations and talks with my father had made me uncommonly aware. My own were made out of pieces of wooden cigar boxes with toothpicks for masts and paper sails. My dog, Massie, watched the events with her own simulated interest until she picked up her leash to take me for a walk.

While I was still in our local elementary school, my mother made me take out Massie every morning at six, followed by at least a half an hour's piano practice. She was a tough teacher and also taught other children in our neighbourhood piano and violin. When I was thirteen, I finally rebelled and was allowed to quit piano provided that I continue with another instrument. So, at Mam's prompting, I switched to mandolin, with my mother again as my teacher because mandolin has the same string arrangement as a violin with which, of course, she was familiar. After a few years, I quit mandolin because I thought it was a girl's instrument and started guitar, which thereafter has always remained my instrument. I played mainly classical music. If I were given the opportunity to relive my life on this planet, I'd be a musician – most likely a mediocre but dedicated violinist.

Apart from Sinterklaas on the fifth of December and New Year's Eve, we rarely had any organized get-togethers. Christmas on December 25th was a religious family affair for most of our friends. Both my father, with a Christian Reformed background, and my mother, once Catholic, had given up their religions a long time ago on philosophical grounds and, while they did not bring us up as atheists, they did not influence their boys in respect of religion. However, my mother did insist that I join our girl Stien in attending the mass in the large Catholic church in Wassenaar early Christmas morning until Stien told my mother that she didn't want to take me along any more because I waved at the choir boys and made faces at them. I then had to go to Sunday school but dropped out after brother Nap discovered that one of my pious classmates had glued a damaged rare stamp of Curaçao and then traded it with me. I disliked both the masses and Sunday school.

As a toddler and before my doubts about religion, I contrived by myself to pray to God every night under my blanket so that my brothers wouldn't find out. I prayed that my parents and brothers would all live eighty years, as well as my dog and cat, but that God shouldn't bother about my Frisian grandmother Berendina (the origin of my second name, Berend) because she bossed me around. As mentioned, Opemoeke lived in The Hague and walked every day about an hour to the beach to sit on a bench and watch the waves. She was always dressed in a long black gown and had a golden cap. She didn't know anything about cholesterol but lived ninety-six years notwithstanding. Except for Opemoeke and Tante Rens in The Hague, our little family in Wassenaar did not have much contact with any other members of the Ages clan or of my mother's family. My parents had several intimate friends in their own fields of interest, my brothers seemed to favour sporty girlfriends over cousins and nieces, and I had my own playmates.

Frits was named after Opa and my father, Frederik Jelte. Nap's name was actually Jan Adriaan, not after anybody, but we all called him Nap, short for Napoleon, except when he was a boy, when my parents called him Pip. Brothers Frits and Nap were very bright but

were both too impatient to spend several years of higher education
to enter some technical or scientific field. They were dedicated to
sport – water polo, horseback riding, sailing, and field hockey – and
they both excelled. They started to play bridge with our neighbours
in Wassenaar, the van Calcars. Unfortunately, after a few raucous
sessions at her house, Mrs. van Calcar complained to my mother
that they were welcome separately but not together because they
were troublemakers and didn't take the game very seriously. So
Frits and Nap both stayed away and didn't lose any sleep over their
dismissal. Frits went to a nautical school in Scheveningen near The
Hague and became a mate (deck officer) with the Nederland Line.
There was no Dutch conscription, but during the war he was a chief
officer of troopships and freighters with the Allies in various war
zones. Nap, a journalist, set up the underground newspaper *Het
Parool* in The Hague and was one of the first members of the Dutch
resistance to enter the German military compound in The Hague
to be present at the German capitulation. Both brothers constantly
lived in high gear during the war years, but survived.

As a little boy of six to ten years, I had a tough time satisfying
my demanding and ambitious big brothers, who at times made me
feel I had three fathers. They never seemed to get tired of teaching
their kid brother many things. Frits, the seaman, showed me the
constellations at night and tried to explain the movement of the
moon. He also taught me how to ride a bike. Nap got me interested
in chess, checkers and collecting stamps. As a press representative
of KLM airlines, he brought home photographs of KLM planes and
he "helped" me write letters to major shipping companies asking for
posters. An enormous poster of the Queen Mary was the pride of
my room. As an apprentice and junior officer with the Nederland
Line, Frits let me come on board his ship after a trip to the then-
Dutch East Indies and I caught cockroaches in the ship's galley to
be traded at school for marbles or cigar bands. Unlike stamps, cigar
bands had no commercial value, but the Dutch youth appeared to
have their own standards.

Apart from our dog Massie, of course, my best friends and
playmates in those years were the boys my age of neighbourhood

families with similar interests to ours. Of those, I'd especially like
to mention Willem Thijsse and Johan Huibregtse. Around 1930,
Willem's family and my own were neighbours for a couple of years,
living in the outskirts of The Hague close to the beach where we
all spent many happy summer weekends. Willem's father, a civil
engineer, was at that time director of a hydraulic model built in
a shed south of The Hague; I think it modelled the tides in the
Zuiderzee. On some Sundays, he took Willem and me along in his
car to show us the model. These Sundays were always very special
to both Willem and me because of the excitement of being in an
automobile, a rarity in those days. Willem's father became director
of the Delta Werken, a spectacular project to block off the southern
estuaries of the Netherlands with flood barriers after the floods in
1953.

The entire Thijsse family was very musical. The three brothers
– Hans, Jaap and Willem – played every Sunday morning at home
in a string quartet with their father, sometimes attended by their
grandfather, Jac P. Thijsse, a well-known botanist. The Thijsses and
the Ages parents regularly attended performances of the Residentie
Orkest in Scheveningen until one evening both tired husbands
fell asleep during a performance, forcing their angry wives to go
without them from then on. Willem went to sea after the war and
ended up as a manager of container traffic in Cape Town. Upon
his retirement, he became a cellist with the symphony orchestra in
that city.

Johan Huibregtse was my schoolmate throughout elementary
school and the gymnasium. His father was head of a local high
school and his mother was a teacher. He became a lawyer while
his brothers taught Latin and Greek at the University of Leiden.
Willem Thijsse and Johan Huibregtse both married young and have
large families in different parts of the world. They have never met
but both have visited me in Victoria a few times, where I've lived
for many years. We are in regular e-mail contact and both sup-
plied memories, facts and anecdotes during the writing of these
memoirs.

Not only my two brothers, but our entire family was very much

involved in sports, particularly water sports. My mother once gave
my father a very beautiful little sail boat for his birthday – a *jol*
called Duikelaar (a diving bird), again paid for by the proceeds of
one of her books. Much to the annoyance of the rest of the family,
he spent part of the summer scraping and varnishing his boat rather
than having her in the water. Frits, Nap and my father were all
very strong swimmers, familiar with the treacherous tidal currents
along our sea shore. Almost every summer, my father or one of my
brothers had to swim out quite far to rescue someone (usually an
unsuspecting visitor from the interior) who had got caught in the
strong ebbflow between the submerged bars and had tried to struggle back against the current.

In the winter, the water was too cold for swimming and beaches
were deserted. Father Jelte then took long walks along the shore
and occasionally met Queen Wilhelmina with her court-lady, also
on a beach walk away from their royal duties. They had some pleasant conversations. Then he would come home and we had to hear
all about "Willemien" until my mother told him that she had heard
enough about Willemien.

If Mam was not teaching music or writing, she would be out
cycling or taking long walks on the beach or riding at our local
manège. Nap and Mam both participated in dressage shows in the
same manège a few times every winter. My father gave up on horses
after he was thrown once and broke his arm in two places. As for
Frits, though he was at sea before and during the war, he had a
friend near Boston with a large stable, and when he was on leave in
between convoys, he'd travel there and ride, even participating in a
tough cross-country. I had to wait until my immigration to Canada
to start riding lessons in 1955 with the Carleys in Victoria.

Surprisingly, neither Frits nor Nap seemed to get the hang of
skating even though they spent an entire winter near frozen lakes in
Switzerland. My father took me to the ice when I was barely six years
old. Unlike my slow progress in other sports, I almost immediately
caught on, much to my father's delight and my mother's concern.
After one extremely cold night in the winter of 1930, I teamed up
with three young brothers – Erik, Frits and Bartje Oosterbaan. The

oldest at ten, Erik was the proud owner of a pair of all-steel speed
skates, the envy of every boy. Speed skates in those days consisted
of a layered steel blade set in a wooden frame that was strapped to
two pairs of socks or *klompsokken*. These were leather inserts in
wooden shoes; shoes would have been too rigid. Bartje, age six like
me, came once to our door without his skates and asked my mother
if "Alard would come to play," while his older brothers were hiding
behind the hedge. Mam was not to be fooled, telling Bartje that the
ice wasn't safe yet and that Alard had to stay home, upon which my
father came dashing down the stairs and told her to let me go. So
off I went with the three Oosterbaan boys. We wanted to be the first
ones to skate "under the bridge," a bridge across a canal well north
of Wassenaar where the funnelled northeast wind overnight had
kept the ice still too thin to support an adult but thick enough, we
figured, for a couple of six year olds after a very fast start. It didn't
work and it was a long way home, soaking wet in a freezing wind.

There was good ice nearly every winter in those years, the thirties and forties; unfortunately, the Dutch climate did not escape the
global warming in more recent decennia. During my first years
at the gymnasium in Leiden, I loved to skate to school, one hour
each way, following a network of frozen canals. I remember walking on the beach with one of my brothers during a cold spell and
stepping around large blocks of sea-ice along the high water line.
We found many oiled birds, killed by the careless bilge-cleaning of
passing tankers. The vivid childhood memory of this massacre of
birds dying a horrible death never left me and became a significant
motivation in my work to help prevent oil spills after I joined the
Institute of Ocean Sciences in Canada.

Father Jelte and mother Leid getting married

Jelte (left) with his buddy engineers

Mam writing a novel

Mam and her guitar with dog Massie

Mam with her zither

Stien with mandoline

Brother Frits and new banjo

Stien's dad with French horn

Frits (16, nautical school) with Alard (5)

Nap (20) and Alard (10) with dog Massie in front of our Kano

Father, Nap and Alard in backyard with puppies

Johan and Alard playing Winnetou and old Shatterhand

Alard dreams at his pond   Willem, Massie, Alard, Piraat   Frits, Mam, Massie in the Wetering

The Wetering (the canal) before the battle with the Fallschirmjäger. The destroyed mill has been rebuilt

Mother and Doddy skating on the Wetering

Mother teasing Sobat Juul

5

FRIESLAND

We went back to school one week after the capitulation and had the finals at our gymnasium in Leiden on June 27th. I failed nearly everything, including the two classical and three modern languages. I was fifteen at the time, the youngest in class, but that was no factor for failing; being "playful" was! As expected, the rector told me to either repeat all of grade four (somewhat equivalent to North America's grade ten) or leave. My parents blamed a mental breakdown due to the war and suggested I change to another, less demanding high school (called HBS in The Netherlands for Hogere Burger School, higher public school), but I insisted on repeating grade four, pointing out that I had not cracked up any more than my classmates and wanted to try again. I confessed that I habitually put off most of my homework before Christmas and then frantically tried to catch up in the spring in order to pass the finals by the skin of my teeth. This time, the events during the spring had interrupted my schedule and I got caught off guard. I had kept my parents unaware of the tough curriculum of a gymnasium, where all the teachers have a doctorate. The HBS is a year shorter and does not teach classical languages. Perhaps I was too young and playful to appreciate Ovid's "Ars Amandi" and Homer's "άνδρα πολυτροπον," but I respected my teachers too much to drop out.

My parents went along with my intentions to repeat the fourth grade and also decided to send me off to a farm in Friesland for the summer rather than have me hang around in Wassenaar and experiment with unexploded war material with my friends. Train traffic was back to normal after the capitulation and they travelled to the village of Grouw in the centre of the province without delays. My parents arranged for my room and board at a farm outside the village and, during my three remaining years at the gymnasium, I went to Grouw almost immediately after the final exams and often again before Christmas.

Although my father was born and raised in Friesland (in De Lemmer), his Lemster Frisian did not agree well with the Grouwster dialect, according to my mother. She detected a somewhat harsh Dutch influence in my father's Frisian, which I thought made sense because of the trading between Amsterdam and De Lemmer across the Zuiderzee several hundred years ago. My father didn't argue because he didn't know much about this aspect and wisely left the issue to her friends in the music world. De Lemmer and Grouw are thirty kilometres apart.

I arrived in Grouw on July 11th and, after an hour's walk from the small railway station well outside the village, found a friendly villager who took me to a landing at the edge of the village where I blew a horn to alert the farm across the canal to fetch me with their rowboat. I was picked up by a row boat with a broadly grinning guy who introduced himself as Tjeerd Snoek and rowed me across to the farm. Later, when I had learned to walk and run in wooden shoes, Tjeerd mentioned that he had been amused at what they call in Friesland *stêds klean*, or city clothes, meaning my buttoned blue jacket and polished shoes, straight from civilized Wassenaar.

At the farm, I met his mother, Haakje Snoek, who owned the farm with her two sons, Tjeerd, nineteen, and Douwe, in his early

Grouw ("ferry" to Seinpolle farm), view from Seinpollo

twenties and much more serious than his fun-loving younger brother. I also shook hands with a long-time family friend, Japik, who lived on the farm to help out and look after the administration. Except for Japik, they all could speak Dutch but, at my request, kept speaking Frisian. They switched to some Dutch words only when I became totally lost in the conversation, which was often.

The Seinpôlle, a relatively small farm with ten Holstein milk cows, consisted of a house, a hay stack and a stall all under one straw roof. In the living area were a day room, or living room, and a *krease keamer*, a "nice" room which would only be unlocked on Sunday for an afternoon tea with visiting neighbours. The word *kreas* in Frisian stands for almost anything beautiful; for instance, a *kreas famke* is a beautiful girl.

During the first weeks in the Seinpôlle, I slept in a box bed in the wall of the day room. The box bed with its large doors was a contraption which I'd never seen anywhere in Holland, where I used to sleep under a wide-open window summer and winter. The bed was built for a guest who could shut the doors if the day room was too noisy, but I was relieved when Haakje offered to let me sleep with the family in the loft upstairs. There was no bathroom. As a teenager, I idolized the Norwegian explorer Amundsen and followed his custom to toughen up with cold showers. At the Seinpôlle, I had to be content with a pump near the cowshed, to the merriment of the Snoek family. (I think Amundsen was right, and it was an emotional experience to visit his cairn in Gjoa-havn in later years when I was participating in a survey of the Arctic.) The farm's outhouse was a busy place in the summer because the cow stalls were occupied by campers, who quite often decorated the outhouse walls with patriotic graffiti such as

wat zullen we ons gelukkig voelen
als we't vuil weer weg zien spoelen

which loosely translates as "how happy we will be when the filth is washed away," with an appropriate drawing of a Nazi being booted out. The artist must have occupied the outhouse quite long to complete his message.

The kitchen was a small shed outside, just large enough to

accommodate a wood stove, but not a cook. Haakje had to stand in the open when she cooked, but it didn't seem to faze her one bit. For breakfast we had *sûpenbrij* (buttermilk porridge with barley). Lunch we often had in the fields when we were haying or cleaning ditches and ate some leftovers. Dinner consisted of steaks with lots of potatoes and a few carrots or beans. Indeed, there was very little variety in meals, but we were too hungry and tired to notice. I have never come across more primitive cooking facilities anywhere, not even while living in tents while surveying the north boundary of Saskatchewan during the winter in 1954, when we existed happily on pancakes and caribou meat that we shared with two dog teams.

A unique aspect of this typically Frisian farm was the way the animals were treated. The cows had names, girl's names, such as Sietske, Janke and Hinke, and their names were carefully painted on name plates above their stalls. In the spring, the cows were let out into the fields near the farm for the summer and it was quite an experience to watch them celebrate their freedom, jumping around and locking horns in sheer exuberance. During the summer, the herd was moved from one grazing field to another, usually by barge. I understood that several of these fields were rented from the local Protestant church, some for grazing and others for haying. Tjeerd and I spent a few weeks transporting hay with a barge that we punted along the canal to the haystack in the Seinpôlle. In the fall, the cows had to be moved back to their stalls, which took several hours of utter confusion. Each cow somehow knew exactly where to find her own stall, but had to push her way past other cows who were trying to do the same thing until they finally settled down. It was a fascinating experience to watch these otherwise docile animals act like human beings fighting for their own niche in society.

Another fascinating episode of life at the farm was the birth of a calf. The neighbouring farmers would traditionally gather to watch the veterinarian and help with the delivery. The local vet invited me sometimes to accompany him on his trips after I had indicated my interest in that profession. One night, we all had to sit around for hours before the delivery, which was carried out with a small tackle.

The trips with the country vet, Mr. de Jong, did not always follow the same routine. One early winter morning, he came by with his motorboat and woke me up to assist him with an operation that few farmers ever witnessed or would have wanted to witness. A young cow in a nearby field had calved too early for her age, panicked and jumped in an ice-covered ditch with the upper body of the drowned calf under the thin ice with the hind part still in the womb. The cow had given up trying to climb back but was still alive when we arrived. The ice was less than a centimetre thick and a low, gloomy haze was hanging over the field in the semi-darkness. Mr. de Jong told me to stay and comfort the animal and ran back to his boat to collect his tools, including a sort of bicycle chain with sharp teeth. He guided the toothed chain around the calf's body inside the womb and then together we sawed the body in two, each of us holding a chains end with one hand and supporting ourselves with the other hand. We pulled the two halves out and then helped the cow out of the hole in the bloodied ice. The animal jumped up and scurried away as if nothing had happened. Mr. de Jong assured me, his shocked volunteer apprentice, that all was well, although I did not understand why a cow about to calve would be left out in the field in the winter. I didn't see the owner. It wouldn't have been tolerated by the Snoek family. Mr. de Jong's wife and son were also veterinarians and the family was highly respected by the tightly knit community.

Around Christmas, the canals and lakes in Friesland normally did not freeze over long and hard enough to support speed skating, but in January, 1942 there was one marathon with one thousand skaters in the race and four thousand in the "tour." It was a national event followed by the entire country. The two-hundred kilometre marathon, *elf stedentocht*, covers eleven towns in Friesland. I had hoped to participate some day, but after skating the shorter, one -hundred kilometre *zestien dorpentocht*, also in Friesland, I left the "real" marathon to the experts.

In the summer, Haakje kept me busy rowing people to and from the village for ten cents a person and an additional five cents for a bike, with a substantial tip if my fare was a farmer, high on Frisian *genever*. I also helped Tjeerd and Douwe bring in the hay or do repairs around the farm. On Saturdays, if the cows were still in their stalls, we did our *sturtwaskje* chores, washing the cow's tails. This activity created much merriment among the Dutch people in a cheese farm near Salmon Arm in British Columbia, when I asked them during a visit if their cattle had their tails washed, too. The owner, also an immigrant from Holland, gathered a couple of farm-hands recently arrived from North Holland and told them to "meet this guy from Friesland where they spend their Saturdays washing the asses of their cattle." All had a good laugh. They were familiar with the Frisian custom.

We sailed on Sundays in the schouw, a popular Frisian class of sailboats, or watched the spectacular *skûtjesilen* (large sail-freight-ers). Sunday evenings, Tjeerd and I cycled to a *merke* (fair) in some nearby village to win prizes at a shooting gallery and return decorated with roses; or, upon request, Tjeerd played accordion and I played mandolin for a sing-a-long or dance of campers at the Seinpôlle, which was always a hit.

Sailing in Friesland with its many canals was tricky in those years because almost nobody enjoyed the luxury of an outboard motor. Approaching a bridge, we had to make very short tacks against the wind or, going downwind, we had to stand by, turn-ing into the wind, and blow our horn, alerting the bridge keeper to partly raise the bridge. I tried to avoid this hassle by having my mother's kayak shipped from Wassenaar to Grouw. I designed a small sail, side boards and a rudder and one day set sail to Sneek, a water sport centre ten kilometres from Grouw. Unfortunately, a strong gust in the middle of a five-kilometre-long lake near Sneek capsized the boat and it took me a long time to straighten things out, particularly since the paddle had drifted away and I had to swim for it in the absence of other boats. Having overcome these inconveniences, I made it to Sneek all right but had to kayak back to Grouw because the wind had gone down. The return trip in the evening made me realize that the shore line looks altogether different after dark. Without a map and a light or the lessons of seafaring brother Frits to find Polaris to locate true north, I kept getting lost trying to cross the lake to the canal. I finally paddled into its entrance by sheer luck. It must have been well after midnight when I found the Seinpôlle where a concerned Haakje was still waiting with supper.

When I later told my parents, my father wasn't the least bit critical of all my blunders, perhaps because he himself had a history of misadventures. As a young man, he once designed an ice boat in his hometown of De Lemmer together with his adventurous buddy, the mayor's son. Neither one was familiar with the aerodynamics of a sail – e.g., that an ice boat can actually outrun the wind. They set out on a lake near the town and almost immediately crashed on a barrier. They were picked up unconscious and, according to my father, the largest piece of the wreck was no more than a couple of decimetres long. My own adventure provided my mother with another story for her Dutch children's book, *Frankie van Frank*. She could have called it *Alard van Jelte*.

Perhaps the most intriguing virtue of this province was the absence of German police or military almost anywhere, particularly in the later years of the occupation, when elsewhere many unsuspecting young men were trapped in streets and houses to be sent to German labour camps or taken hostage after the resistance eliminated a Nazi. It was a perfect area to hide because one could see the enemy approach in a car or motorboat from a long distance in this very flat country. Moreover, there were hardly any Nazi collaborators to point out hiding places to the police. The odd German patrol boat showed up in the canals and lakes, but their noisy diesel engines gave us ample time to scramble and hide in the reeds along the shore. The boats were usually manned by members of the Kriegs marine, who were known for their reluctance to do this kind of work, as my own experience with these raids attests on page 96.

In the winter, the frozen canals and lakes were crowded with skaters, and *razzias* (roundups of men) on ice would be far from one's mind. Similar conditions existed in other provinces. We never spotted a German uniform on skates anywhere during the winter.

Shortly before my second summer at the Seinpôlle, the oldest son Douwe got married. He and his wife Feikje moved to a houseboat tied up to the embankment nearby. My father gave them a large Junghaus wall clock as a wedding gift, only to find out that the waves from passing boats threw the clock's movements off beat or stopped it altogether. The clock had to be transferred to the *krease keamer.* (I should have remembered this problem years later when I took my cuckoo clock on the survey vessel the *William Stewart* when we charted the lively Hecate Strait on the west coast of British Columbia and I had to pack it away, to the relief of my shipmates.)

Tjeerd also got married, to *kreas famke* Hinke, the stunningly beautiful daughter of a neighbour farmer. They had two *bern* (children) and eventually moved to nearby Akkrum where Tjeerd became a bridge keeper. With his accordion, he joined a popular ensemble of musicians, while Hinke became a member of an equally active folk dancing group. A few years ago, Tjeerd had a stroke and passed away, the last member of the original Seinpôlle family. During my last visit to Friesland in the fall of 2005, I was sad to notice the change in scenery made by asphalt roads, houses replacing farms and, worst of all, the ugly but "efficient" giant windmills.

6

THE GYMNASIUM

After my first summer in Grouw, the return trip to Wassenaar was a bit depressing. It was nice to be home again with my parents, but instead of waking up to the lowing of the cows waiting to be milked, I had to listen to German soldiers marching in the street below my window and singing that they were on their way to fight England.

Denn wir fah - ren, denn wir fah-ren, denn wir fah - ren ge-gen Enge-land

Then they would halt for a moment to go boom-boom with their heels on the pavement and continue with the next verse. It puzzled me how grown-up men could be motivated to take part in this childlike exercise and I wondered if their girlfriends in Germany had ever watched.

I had not been looking forward to repeating the fourth grade courses all over again, although I was reunited with classmates who had repeated earlier class levels. The gymnasium building in Leiden at that time was only a few years old – a marvel of architecture in a location well outside the centre of the city. Most of our classrooms had an unobstructed view of large fields and a canal. Like other gymnasia in the Netherlands, it was and probably still is not a private school. Elementary students graduating from their grade six had to pass an exam to be admitted to grade one gymnasium. A student completing grade four gymnasium could choose between an α and a β curriculum to continue the two last years, the α direction specializing in classical languages and cultures, and the β class in math and physics with less emphasis on the classical languages. Most of my classmates were sons or daughters of professors or people involved in education. For instance, the father of my friend Johan Huibregtse was head of a high school, his mother a teacher and his two older brothers were both teaching Latin and Greek. Johan and I were classmates throughout elementary school in Wassenaar and at the gymnasium in Leiden to grade four, which I had to repeat. As for grades five and six, I chose the β option and graduated in 1943. The β option later allowed me to skip first year science at the University of British Columbia.

Politically, during my years at the gymnasium, only three of the three hundred students were known to be sympathetic to the Nazis. A girl in our fifth and sixth grades had one German parent. She was once seen walking with a member of the SS and was immediately branded as a Nazi – maybe a member of the Gestapo! A girl in our class asked her about it but did not get a straight answer, and from then on she was ostracized, not just by our class, but by the entire school, for two years. During recess, she walked alone. She did not betray anybody. Another student was a member of the Dutch Nazi party, the NSB. He once asked the teacher to be allowed to address the class. He told us that, indeed, he was a member of the NSB and that he had no intention of changing his views, but that he would never betray anyone. The grade six class was impressed by his forthright speech and respected him from then on.

As far as we know, there were no betrayals by any of the students at our gymnasium throughout the occupation years. Apart from a fist fight between two twelve-year-old grade one students, there were no physical altercations either. One of the two kids involved in that fight was the son of the newly appointed and disliked mayor of Leiden, a member of the NSB. The mayor's son was badly beaten and left with a bloodied face, to the enjoyment of the large crowd of older students. His father did not retaliate, possibly because he had already made himself unpopular by ordering the teachers and students of all high schools to attend a show of the Reichs Arbeitsdienst, a labour service, essentially a predecessor of military service. Other high schools in Leiden, like the HBS, had refused to cooperate after the parents had jointly written a letter saying that they did not want their children to attend such a display. All parents of high school students, including mine, subsequently received a note from the mayor saying that they had in that aspect "ceased control over their children" whose attendance at such displays was to be compulsory.

The Arbeitsdienst shows became a great source of friction between the high schools and the Nazi administration. The staff of our gymnasium had an early morning meeting on November 10th, 1941 to decide if they would follow the example of the HBS schools. During the secret meeting, they locked the students out. Rather than wait outside, we all started to march through Leiden, three hundred students singing and shouting all over town, giving the impression that we were demonstrating against the Nazis. When we returned after a couple of hours, our teachers were livid. Our con-rector and math teacher, Dr. de Jong, went from class to class to chastise us, but we suspected that our teachers had yielded to the Nazi mayor because they had decided to send us to the *Arbeitsdienst* show. I did not go and my father was summoned to the office of the rector and returned without revealing anything but obviously supporting the teaching staff.

Judging from the occasional remarks by our teachers, we assumed that there were no Nazi sympathizers among them, but I was never clear about Dr. de Jong's views until I found out. We had a framed picture of Queen Wilhelmina hidden behind one of the curtains shielding the windows. During a math test, de Jong wandered around the classroom. I watched him walk past the curtain hiding the portrait. He casually moved the curtain aside and spotted it, then moved the curtain back and continued his stroll. Someone must have told him about it. The portrait remained there until we graduated, and Dr. de Jong was okay.

On January 3rd, 1944, a Dutch Nazi administrator, Diederix, was shot in Leiden. The next afternoon, de Jong was picked up together with a school teacher and a doctor. While being taken to a building of the Feld Gendarmerie (German police), they were shot in the

back and left to die on the street. The perpetrators were arrested after the liberation of Holland and either imprisoned or executed. They had been members of the notorious Silbertanne action, set up by Rauter, head of the Sicherheits Polizei. The group aimed to kill three prominent and known anti-Nazi members of a community to avenge the murder of a local Nazi. The people targeted by Rauter's group would be marked with a sketch of a silver fir behind their name in the town's register. Rauter was executed in The Hague after the liberation. Dr. de Jong had been targeted because of his prominence, unbeknownst to any of us, in resisting attempts by the Nazis to take over the administration of universities and schools, not only in Leiden but also elsewhere in the country.

A building across from the gymnasium on the Fruinlaan in Leiden had been appropriated by the German military command shortly after their arrival in May, 1940. There had not been any interaction between the German occupants and the teachers or students at the gymnasium until one day in the fall of 1941. Two German officers tried to enter the Fruinlaan on their bicycles just when the students were dismissed at the school and, as usual, milled around outside. Shouting *"los, los"* ("make way," the officers tried to force their way through and cycled into a couple of kids, promptly creating a hostile mob of hundreds of students pushing and shouting. The two Germans panicked, grabbed three of the senior students and forced the surprised boys inside the building, locking the doors on the screaming mob outside. According to one of the three boys, my classmate Paul van Schaik, they were led to the commandant to be interrogated. The commandant appeared to be a jovial man with little interest in the affair. He put the boys at ease and went into a long discussion about various topics. After four years of German at the gymnasium, the boys felt the exchange went all right. They were released later in the afternoon, without even having to give their names. At school the next morning, they were treated like real heroes.

The three students had been lucky to run into a high-ranking German official with a sense of humour, perhaps someone who himself had teenage children back in Germany. I had a different encounter a few weeks earlier. While cycling home from school along the highway to Wassenaar, I was overtaken by three "brown-shirts" with swastikas on their sleeves, member of the NSDAP, the National Sozialistische Deutsche Arbeiterpartei. One of the goons pulled up beside me and ripped off my red-white-and-blue Dutch bicycle flag, then threw me down on the pavement. All three jumped off their bikes to start a fight. Rather than being scared, I was too flabbergasted to attempt to stand up to the three of them but, fortunately, a group of road workers who had watched the attack from across the highway immediately came to my aid. The three Nazis quickly jumped back on their bikes and took off. Neither my very solid old Bailey bicycle (without a gearshift but with new tires) nor I sustained any damage in this rather commonplace exchange. I attached another little Dutch flag to the frame with a steel wire instead of a string. I later removed this rather conspicuous pennon to prevent my loyal indispensable bike from being noticed during a bicycle roundup by the Germans.

An unexpected problem facing the gymnasium administration was its endeavour to introduce Italian as a non-credit course. The Italian consulate in The Hague was approached to send one of its members to our school to teach interested students one evening per week. I thought it was a great idea, not only because of our family's Latin and French background, but also because my parents had studied Italian and we still had several textbooks and a dictionary at home. Many students enrolled and the Italian consulate was most cooperative.

During the introduction of the Italian gentleman by one of our teachers, a student in the front row of the class turned around and said, "Die meneer draagt een fasces op zijn revers" ("The guy's wearing a fasces on his lapel," the fasces being the Italian equivalent of the German swastika). The students were furious. Our own teacher pleaded with us to mind our manners, but the class remained hostile and the course had to be cancelled. I thought the class overreacted and should have let him teach at least a few sessions, even if he would become involved in a dialogue about fascism. After all, he wasn't wearing a swastika! What also came to mind was the attitude of my parents towards the two young German paratroopers billeted at our house after the invasion of May, 1940.

One of the most bizarre attempts of the Nazi regime to manipulate the young minds of students was to rewrite our textbooks, for instance, by striking out any reference to German misdemeanours in earlier wars or even to the Dutch Queen. Our grade four chemistry book had a page dealing with properties of chlorine and mentioned that the Germans were the first nation to use it in the first world war, during the battle at Yperen in Belgium. We had to hand in this textbook to have the page cut out and replaced by exactly the same page without that sentence. Among other censored words was an expression in our French textbook, *Leve de Koningin* (long live the Queen) and the French *Vive la Reine*, which became *Leve de Koning* and *Vive le Roi*, as if the owners of these books did not promptly restore the original words: Leve de Koningin!

The *entjüdung* (elimination of Jews) of Holland by the Nazis started in 1941 and continued until the end of the war in 1945. It did not spare our gymnasium. A couple of Jewish students went into hiding (one of them apparently in the house of our English teacher, Dr. Prins) and surfaced after the liberation, but a girl in front of me in grade four did not come to class one morning and never showed up again during and after the occupation. Lilly Meiler was a very attractive and charming, conspicuously Jewish girl. At the time of her disappearance, we had no idea why and only learned after the war about the transport, between July, 1942 and September, 1944 through Camp Westerbork in the Eastern Netherlands, of one hundred thousand Dutch Jews to the gas chambers in Auschwitz and other extermination camps. If she had been in hiding, she would certainly have contacted one of her classmates after the war, as did other Jewish students. She did not, and we have our misgivings.

Absenteeism was not unusual and wasn't necessarily related to sickness in those years. Sometimes a student had to go into hiding during a local *razzia* (a German roundup) or had been involved in a resistance coup. I once noticed a classmate across from my desk put a small pistol in his desk for whatever reason. I asked him about it and, as expected, he told me it was just a toy for his kid brother's birthday. He left with his "toy" after school and disappeared for a few days. It must have been quite a birthday party!

There was not much social life among us. We had two student associations, *Uno sumus Animo* (non-religious) and *Spes* (Christian Reformed) with some theatre and alcohol-free outings. The former praeses (president) of the U.S.A., Okki van der Plas, went on to study engineering in Delft where he joined the resistance. Together with five other engineering students, Okki successfully blew up a train and patrol boat near Rotterdam. I learned from the newspaper that all six were court martialled and executed by the Germans on May 20, 1943.

Physical education only took one hour a week and there were no sport activities. During recess, we didn't play any games but walked around the building in small groups and discussed politics or the latest local events, which were many. For the students commuting from Wassenaar, there was no lack of exercise because we cycled in whenever feasible – at times an hour against a strong north wind in the morning. In the winter, as I mentioned, some of us skated along the frozen canals, which was a joy.

In the classroom, we covered our benches with our own little

cushions, not because we were softies but because we had to save
pants and skirts, which were so hard to get. Of course, there was
the odd cushion fight and the frantic clean-up of floating feathers
and kapok before the next lecture. Students from outside Leiden
had lunch in a meeting room around a horseshoe-shaped table
with one of our volunteer teachers at the head. We brought our
own sandwiches and drank a cup of hot chocolate courtesy of the
gymnasium. There were no vending machines, of course. Saturday
and Wednesday were half days for all levels. Most of my classmates
spent evenings studying until 10 pm. With my confounded inabil-
ity to pay attention to lectures in class, I certainly did myself. Of
course, the lack of TV in our homes in those years was a significant
factor in getting our course work done.

When our class graduated in the spring of 1943, there were no
options to continue on by attending a university unless we signed a
declaration of loyalty to the Nazi regime. As far as I know nobody
did, mostly because Jewish professors were not allowed to teach
any more – nor would we have, even had they been allowed. We
celebrated our graduation in an ice cream saloon in Leiden.

On June 11th, 1988, I attended the fifty-year lustrum (anniversary)
of our gymnasium at the Fruinlaan in Leiden. Since my graduation
in 1943, I had not visited the school and it was quite an experience
to meet several of my classmates again and reminisce about our
life in the forties. The curriculum had changed significantly and
seemed to aim more at the fun of learning than at the more rigid
and possibly more productive approach of our years.

The lifestyle of the students had also changed. Instead of wearing
the conventional jacket, pants and a tie, the boys now were dressed
in blue jeans and all sorts of wild T-shirts, while the girls' coat and
skirt had been replaced by blue jeans and a blouse or sweater. I'd say
that the dress code had improved. Then some of the young teenage
students who had done a lot of work for the event were rewarded
with . . . bottles of Bols gin! I wondered how our Canadian Mounties
would have reacted to this kind of treat.

Four of us old-timers continued the party that night in a *gezellig*
restaurant in the heart of the city (*gezellig* is uniquely Dutch. The

closest translation would be something like "socially enjoyable"). I had been in touch with only one or two close former mates with whom I still communicate via e-mail. Tineke, Annetje, Ben Crul and I had many things to talk about and it surprised me how much the two women still lived in the occupation years, while neither Ben nor I gave the issue a lot of attention any more, possibly because both of us had spent a large part of our post-war life abroad. Ben worked in the Caribbean as an engineer before his retirement, while I was at sea and later emigrated to Canada.

After the lustrum, several of our 1943 graduates kept meeting annually at the house of Hélène Nauta-Barge in Leiden and a few times at Sietze Bouwer's in Soest, not far from the house where I was born in 1924. Although most of us are now around eighty years old, I couldn't help noticing that the women among us, without exception, looked and acted much younger than the men.

Graduating class, Gymnasium (Spring 1943)

7

AMSTERDAM ~ THE NAUTICAL COLLEGE

So there we were, happy to have left behind us three stressful years of trying to remain focused on our courses in a very distracting environment. But what now? In peaceful years, most of the α and β graduates would have started to prepare for a university. Such a move would now, in 1943, be considered a betrayal of the students who had refused to sign a declaration of loyalty to the Nazi administration and of the professors who had resigned in protest of the dismissal of their Jewish colleagues. More pragmatically, how would a future employer in the Netherlands, or perhaps elsewhere, react to an application by a university graduate who had obtained his or her degree during the occupation?

Everyone in our graduating class tried at all costs not to be snared by the Arbeitseinsatz, the labour mobilization, particularly in the occupied territories, to replace the millions of German men and women in military service throughout Europe. Many new graduates went into hiding (*onderduiken* in Dutch, meaning "diving"), or enrolled in technical schools, which had not yet been closed by the Germans. A letter from the school's director confirming the student's registration had so far been sufficient to obtain an *Ausweis*, a certificate exempting the bearer from the Arbeitseinsatz.

Another cunning way to escape the German labour dragnet was to repeat the graduating class but register in the other option – certainly not a wasted year because of the totally different subject matter. So far, the Germans had not interfered with high school education. Johan Huibregtse managed to end up with an α as well as a β diploma, then had to go into hiding with friends in Wassenaar until the end of the war in 1945, after which he took up law.

I had no intention of enrolling in a university even if there had not been a war. I had been dreaming about becoming a fighter pilot, preferably flying a Spitfire! However, the Dutch airforce had been completely destroyed and, under the circumstances, I decided to follow the family tradition and go to sea. I applied to the Kweekschool voor de Zeevaart, or KvdZ (the nautical college), in Amsterdam as early as Christmas, 1942, well aware of the tough competition from other graduates who had no interest in seamanship but were trying to remain exempt from the Arbeitseinsatz.

On May 17th, 1943, two weeks before the written and oral finals at the gym, I was interviewed in Amsterdam by the commandant and the teaching staff of the Kweekschool, followed by a medical exam—altogether, a six-hour event. To my surprise the commandant asked me about my position on the Nazis and I told him. Apparently, all the other applicants had to answer the same question. As far as I know, there were no Nazi sympathizers in our class of about forty students, or in other classes or among the teachers and other staff members.

During a couple of free hours between interview and medical, I had an opportunity to take a walk to the nearby centre of Amsterdam. Strangely enough, I had never been to our capital, the birthplace of my mother. Apart from the odd German Oberlieutenant with his girlfriend and Leica camera, there were no tourists, no sightseeing boats, no guided tours of Amsterdam's red light district or warehouses dating back to its golden age between the seventeenth and eighteenth centuries. There were no ships in the harbour either because its access from the North Sea had been blocked by the Dutch navy's scuttling of our liner *Jan Pieterszoon Coen* at the entrance of the North Sea canal in May, 1940. I visited the Jewish district (a bit hard to define in this cosmopolitan city) and was surprised by the number of Stars of David all around. Jews in Nazi-occupied countries were forced to wear these yellow stars with the word "Jew" written in their local language, e.g., "Jood" in Dutch. I had been under the impression that all our Jewish citizens had by then been transported to German labour camps – death camps as we learned later—or had gone into hiding and disappeared. However, during my short visit, the streets were unaccountably still teeming with obviously Jewish people and I did not see any disruptive Nazi uniforms.

A strange experience was the sound of air raid sirens in the afternoon. Two American fighter bombers skimmed over the houses, barely dodging a couple of church towers. They dropped bombs on a factory in the city's outskirts (the gasworks, according to my diary). In Wassenaar, air raid sirens had not howled for a long time, most likely because of the continuous air activity above our town, the Luftwaffe around the airport at Valkenburg and the R.A.F. and U.S. Air Force interested in the lavish Wassenaar villas occupied by the German top brass.

Impressed by the school as well as the city, I very much hoped to be accepted but had to wait not only for the determination of the interview, but also for the results of the finals at the gymnasium two weeks later.

En route to and from Amsterdam, I noticed a very large crowd at the train station in Leiden saying goodbye to a few men getting on. They were the families of professional Dutch military personnel, among them the mariniers, who had to report to prisoner-of-war camps in Germany. They had been set free after the capitulation of the Dutch forces but, because of the threat of a possible allied invasion, the men had to go to the camps again. Most of them went because they had families to support on a reduced pay, which they would not receive if they went into hiding. The number of professional military personnel was too large for financial support from the resistance, which could only help those who played an important role in the resistance while in hiding.

Whatever might be the results of the interview and the medical, I still had to pass the exams at the gymnasium in the following two weeks in order to graduate and be formally accepted by the KvdZ. The gym's finals, in Greek, Latin, Dutch, French, German, English, Algebra, Geometry, Analytical Trigonometry, Physics, Chemistry and Biology, consisted of written exams as well orals. The orals were attended by professors of the University of Leiden. According to a detailed entry in my diary, our written exam in Dutch was an impromptu essay on suggested topics such as "a child's life: a discovery voyage," a somewhat tired subject; and another one "sua feta habent libelli," which nobody touched because none of us knew what it meant, in spite of our six years of Latin!

Impromptu subjects for a class essay always scared me because at times I could not find inspiration for any of the topics. During an earlier test, while fighting against time, I tried to pick something of my own and then somehow fit it into one of the listed topics. I looked out the window and watched a horse and a calf having a great time playfully chasing each other in a large field behind our school. In the last few minutes before the bell sounded, I wrote a weird fantasy about these two animals, calling the story "What I Saw Out of Our Window." I handed it in, convinced that I had ruined my already shaky record in the Dutch language class. The next day, our teacher for Dutch, Dr. Kloots, met me in the hall with a big grin on his face and told me that he had read the story to a couple of his other classes. I thought he was being sarcastic, but he showed me my mark and it looked like at least my native language wouldn't be a concern any more. Upon further reflection, it occurred to me that the reason for these compulsory topics at the beginning of written exams was to prevent students from preparing their essays well in advance and that my teacher let me get away with it this time because my story was obviously spontaneous.

The written and oral finals started on May 20th and ended on June 1st. There were fifteen candidates for the α diploma and twenty β candidates. We received our results on June 2nd, almost instantly after the last day. There were a few rewrites among the α students but eventually all of us passed, possibly because teachers and professors generously took into consideration the conditions under which we studied and were examined. Almost day and night, armadas of allied bombers passed over Leiden en route to and from the German industrial area of Dordtmund, Essen and Wuppertal, while Spitfires or Mosquitoes visited us regularly to strafe some local target. Then, of course, there was the nagging uncertainty of our future after the exams.

As regards my own accomplishments, I barely scraped through Latin without a rewrite but did well in Greek, which was no surprise. Somehow my romantic young mind associated Latin with the Nazi-like expansionism of the Romans (e.g., Ceasar's de Bello Gallico) while the Greeks (Athens) seemed to favour (and peacefully export) a more creative lifestyle.

On June 2nd, a day after the graduation of our β class, I took my gymnasium diploma to the KvdZ in Amsterdam and received a statement by the commandant confirming my registration at the school. This letter to the administration of the Arbeitseinsatz in The Hague requested my exemption from the Arbeitseinsatz, which had been made compulsory for all men in the Netherlands between eighteen and forty-five. I went to the Arbeitseinsatz office in The Hague with the letter. The office consisted of some old tables and worn-out chairs in a smelly basement occupied by a few men with NSB (Dutch Nazis) badges. There was a group of men standing around, waiting for an interview. In all my innocence, I headed straight for one of the tables, sat down and showed the letter to the man behind the table. He casually glanced at the letter. Then, perhaps at the sight of the word "commandant" below the signature and the fancy letterhead, he marked my Identification card (Persoonsbewijs in Dutch) with a stamp exempting me from the Arbeitseinsatz and politely sent me on my way, past the queue of nervously waiting men. For a while, this stamp proved invaluable when I had to pass roadblocks set up by the German police to apprehend unsuspecting passersby without an *Ausweis* (the stamp) and have them sent to work camps in Germany and elsewhere. Since the majority of the KvdZ students (called *kwekelingen* in Dutch) lived outside Amsterdam and often spent weekends at home, an Ausweis was a necessity on the train between Amsterdam and our homesteads.

The Kweekschool voor de Zeevaart takes pride in being the oldest nautical school in the world. It was established in 1785 by a group of prominent citizens in Amsterdam and patronized by the Dutch Royal House. Over the years, the school has shown considerable flexibility in sharing its courses in navigation with other interests such as the navy and KLM, the Dutch airline. What set the KvdZ apart from other nautical schools in the Netherlands was its offer to high school graduates (HBS 5 years, β six years) to complete all theoretical and practical courses in one year, while the conventional two-year program would still be open to all students having completed the three-year level. Both my gymnasium classmate Ben Crul and I went for the one-year option, and survived. My old friend Willem Thijsse, a lyceum graduate, took the two-year approach and kept smiling all the way. Both one-year and two-year options end up with the same final exams, but the practical seamanship courses might prove a bit more thorough in the longer period of training.

My older brother Frits, with an equivalent of three years of high school, had completed a two-year program at the nautical school in Scheveningen (near The Hague) before the war; as previously mentioned, he was a chief officer in allied convoys from 1940 to 1945.

The KvdZ was a boarding school; tuition, room and board were paid for by my father. We slept in two large dorms, one for the one-year kwekelingen and the other for the two-year students. There were no walls or screens in the dorms and if someone snored, his neighbours had to get up and shake him. Another student kept rolling back and forth in his bed while talking in his sleep and we just left him alone. Of course, there were some dorm raids by the two-year students next door. Because of our alphabetical arrangement, my bed was the first one near the door to be overturned and land on top of me, soon followed by Bakker and Biermans. That's where the raid usually ended because Biermans had been woken up by the noise and Biermans was big and angry. Judging by the nocturnal arguments outside our dorm, the street behind us seemed to be an extension of the red light district and provided us with some entertaining evenings. We opened the windows to shout encouragement to the girls trying to get paid by their clients until the boatswain appeared and told us to turn in. One of the four boatswains was always on night duty, assisted by a senior *kwekeling*.

At 6:00 a.m. on weekdays, the lights went on in our dorm in all their sadistic brightness while the boatswain shouted "Rijze Rijze Rijze!" (Rise!). How could we not? We hurried into our clothes,

scampered down the stairs to the mess room for a slice of bread
with mayonnaise (butter? margarine? Ha! We had gobbled up
our weekly rations of a few cubic centimetres almost immediately
after they were distributed) and a cup of coffee I believe was made
of alder leaves. Then we went to the gym to undress again and run
around for half an hour, showered and headed to our classroom
to study, supervised by the boatswain. After an hour's study, we
had breakfast and made our beds before going to classes for eight
hours of lectures. Lunch breaks were short and, after dinner (usually some kind of hotch potch – mashed potatoes and carrots – and
very popular nutritious pea soup), we went back to class to do our
homework, again supervised by one of the boatswains reading a
book at his desk in front of the class. There was no talking in class
during these study sessions, or doing something not related to our

My Bak at KvdZ . Back row (standing) left to right: Crul, Bakker, Edens, Bierman, Dubiez
Front (kneeling): Ages, van Dalfsen, Bulstra

homework.

Without exception, the theoretical as well as practical sessions in ship construction, design and use of a sextant, shape of propellers, ships engines, meteorology, ocean currents, and theory of tides were very interesting. And then there was the large tackle loft where the boatswains taught splicing, knots, sewing and hemming. They took us out on the boats to sail, row and scull. We also had to go up the mast of a partly square-rigged schooner built on the square below our class rooms, and hoist or trim the sails.

The commandant, Mr. Daan van der Hiel, also taught a course: ship building. When he entered the classroom, we had to stand next to our bench until he signalled that we could sit down again. As in our dorm, I was the one closest to the door and when I saw him approach the door, I had to holler "IN ORDE!" and the class hurried to their seats to stand at attention. This task gave me a taste of power and I couldn't resist the temptation once to give the call well before the commandant was in sight, to the displeasure of my classmates.

"Once more, Ages, and you go over the side when we're rowing."

Upon our arrival at the KvdZ in the late summer of 1943, we had to change into a uniform – white cotton pants and a white shirt with a small necktie in black and a short black jacket with brass buttons (I don't remember if the school also provided us with black shoes). We had to wear this (quite comfortable) outfit all the time, but were not allowed to leave the grounds in uniform after a group of uniformed *kwekelingen* took on a contingent of Dutch Nazis (called W.A.) marching in Amsterdam the year before. Knives and knuckle-dusters were found in some of the boys' sea chests in the dorm and confiscated by the staff.

The boatswains were, perhaps unwittingly, a big factor in restraining this community of restive young men from being provoked into some spontaneous demonstration against the Nazi regime, which might well have led to closure of the KvdZ. Taking turns, at least one of them was with us all the time, day and night, supervising study sessions, meals, even marching us to the swimming pool in the centre of Amsterdam once a week at six in the morning. At noon on Saturdays, we were free to go until Sunday night, but not all of us. The senior boatswain, whom we nicknamed "De Generaal," would take out his nasty little book and read out the names of *kwekelingen* who were going to be detained for part or all of the weekend because of misdemeanours. I got booked once for using my bed as a trampoline just when De Generaal walked in our dorm at bedtime. I also got booked that same weekend for talking after the boatswain blew his whistle and ordered "Bidden" (pray) before our dinner. That weekend, I had to holystone the staircase (scouring it with a special stone) and scrub the floor, but didn't really suffer because I had the whole recreation room for myself for much of the weekend and was soon joined by another weekend prisoner to play snooker and chess. The large, richly furnished recreation room overlooked part of the harbour. We gathered there often and once two dozen of us had had a simultaneous chess game with our physics teacher. I drew.

The unusually tough and sometimes downright silly discipline maintained by the KvdZ staff was recognized by the students as part of the centuries' old tradition (anno 1785) of this magnificent school. We didn't complain; after all, the alternative would be a Nazi work camp or a hiding place in the home of a courageous family. Moreover, we respected the experience and integrity of the school's staff and teachers.

As at all schools in Holland, there were no lessons on Wednesday afternoon, perhaps in exchange for Saturday morning's sessions, and we could saunter about in the city (in our civvies). Some of us once in a while had a beer with the prostitutes nearby, who did not conduct business on Wednesday afternoons either. They seemed to consider us young and green *kwekelingen* as their baby brothers who had to be cautioned against the evils in foreign ports. Their stories were a bit more colourful than the odd lecture on this topic by our chief officer, Mr. Kruisinga.

One Wednesday afternoon, more precisely on the 22nd of March, 1944, I was strolling with a couple of classmates in the main street of Amsterdam, called the Damrak, when we happened to see one of the most spectacular aviation crashes we ever witnessed during

the war. A large fleet of American Flying Fortresses passed over the city at high altitude, noticeable only by flashes of reflected sunlight on their fuselages. They were obviously returning from a daylight bombing raid in Germany. One of the giant bombers suddenly appeared above the centre of the city, flying unusually low. It seemed to wobble, flying through heavy anti-aircraft fire. We noticed some parachutes descending above the city when a crowd of people came running in panic along the Damrak towards us. Then we spotted an enormous wheel following the crowd. It kept shedding sparks and flames until it tipped over in the middle of the Damrak, where it kept burning. The plane, as we learned later, went down on a school about two kilometres west of the Damrak. The crew surrendered to the Germans. Judging by the distance between the rolling wheel and the plane crash, one would assume that the wheel came off when the plane was under anti-aircraft fire. It also looked like the pilot had tried to ditch his aircraft in the water rather than on the school. Fortunately, it was Wednesday afternoon and school was not in session.

The final exams started in late June, 1944, for both our one-year class and the senior two-year level. Our class graduated on July 22nd. We all did well, as might be expected after the rigorous study sessions under the supervision of the boatswains. Sadly, one *kwekeling* in our one-year group, Lammers, did not make it. (I do not know his first name; for whatever reason, boys in Holland at that time did not address each other by their first names, certainly not as school girls did). After being admitted to the school's hospital infirmary, he was sent home in Katwijk (near my hometown Wassenaar), where he died of meningitis. He was buried in Katwijk on February 4th; many of his classmates as well as our commandant attended the funeral. I was one of the pallbearers.

Traditionally, a graduation ceremony would take place on the grounds of the KvdZ, but the commandant notified us that there would be no such congregation and that the diplomas would be mailed to our homes. No reason was given but, of course, an assembly of graduates would almost be an open invitation to the German police (the *Grünen*), who would come to arrest the whole lot of trained cadets and deliver us to the Arbeitseinsatz, likely to the German merchant navy…. We already had a taste of what might be in store for us after we'd completed our training; during the morning of April 29th, the KvdZ had a surprise visit by the Grüne Polizei. One of our classmates, Wijhenke, was giving a seminar in front of the class as part of our training in oral presentations. Facing the window for a few moments, he stopped abruptly. I figured he had lost his cool, but then he mumbled. "De Grünen, daar zijn de Grünen…." Four members of the Grüne Polizei had just walked through the gates and entered the office of the KvdZ gate keeper. We panicked at the thought of a *razzia*, but our teacher, the commandant himself, calmly ordered Wijhenke to continue his talk and gestured to us to stay in our seats. It wasn't a *razzia*, but all of us had to appear in person before the Germans, who had, uninvited, set up shop in the rec room and examined our Ausweises.

They left without any further hassle, but later, around June 30th, during the last days of our exams, the Reichs Kommissar, Seyss-Inquart, demanded the addresses of the parents of all graduates of the KvdZ as well as those of the graduates of other nautical and ships engineering schools in the Netherlands. Schools who did not comply would face closure. Clearly an order from Seyss-Inquart's office itself to locate the graduates was an indication that the Germans were desperately short of trained nautical personnel and that we were running out of loopholes to escape the Arbeitseinsatz. Dr. Seyss-Inquart, the "Reichs-Kommissar für die besetzen Niederländischen Gebiete," was the highest official of the German administration of occupied Holland. He was a lawyer and one of Hitler's protégés after his involvement with the National Socialist coup d'état in Austria on March 11, 1938, leading to the Anschlusz, the annexation of Austria by Germany. Being merely fourteen years old at that time, I was not interested in politics, but I remember that some of my parents' friends, upon their hasty return from turbulent Vienna, had been under the impression that the public opinion in Austria welcomed the annexation, in contrast with other Germanic neighbours.

After his appointment, Seyss-Inquart wasted little time in helping himself to one of the posh villas of Wassenaar left unoccupied after the death of its owner, a baroness. This mansion, called Clingendael, became the social centre of the German top brass. His Austrian wife, Gertrude, soon joined him and supervised the renovation of Clingendael and another villa that he had claimed as an alternative in case the R.A.F. tracked him down in Clingendael. According to an interview with his Dutch butler after the liberation of Holland in 1945, Seyss-Inquart and his wife kept to themselves and were far from extravagant in their entertainment. "Seyss" (popularly known as 6 ¼ in Holland) had a conspicuous limp, sustained by a mountaineering accident in Austria. He was sentenced to death at the Nuremberg trials and executed in October, 1946. I always regarded Seyss-Inquart as an insignificant and somewhat sad semi-intellectual who had marched along behind the swastika, no questions asked. But, in the meantime, we were stuck with the guy and his memorandum to obtain our whereabouts after graduation.

I remember vividly that last summer morning after the final exams at the KvdZ when I lay down on a bench in our square and considered my options to avoid being caught by the Nazis, now that my Ausweis had expired with the end of my attendance at the Kweekschool. I was convinced that the war was not going to be over for quite some time, perhaps one or two years. I wanted to get out. A possibility was to spend a week or so in Wassenaar, sneak my mother's kayak through the dunes at night and hide it near the beach. I would launch it the next evening and paddle westward in the dark, covering about forty kilometres before daylight and staying out of sight until hopefully being spotted by an English patrol boat the next morning. While recently leafing through my diary (1940-44), I actually came across an entry contemplating this effort, one hundred and thirty kilometres shore to shore; coincidentally, that entry was on April 23rd, 1941 when I had failed my gymnasium grade 4. It was a crazy idea, particularly because I was not familiar with the tidal currents.

Others had made similar attempts. Some of them made it; others did not. The two sons of an acquaintance of my father had tried something similar and miraculously managed to carry a small boat through the dunes at night. It had an outboard motor and they had earlier buried a couple of gas tanks in the sand near the beach. When they went to pick up the gas tanks, the German police were waiting for them and they were arrested. The wind had blown the sand away, exposing the tanks. They were not executed but had to spend the rest of the occupation in a labour camp. A more successful attempt was made by an acquaintance at the nautical school in Scheveningen (near Wassenaar) who, after his graduation, became an apprentice on a German vessel in the Baltic. While passing Sweden during the night, he dove over the side and, after a long swim in frigid water, made it to the beach. We lost track of him, but I imagine he would have joined the Dutch navy in England. Then there was a classmate in grade four of our gymnasium who dropped out and travelled south with a friend, both as street musicians. They never made it to Spain, but were picked up in Belgium by the German police, who were at a loss as to what to do with these two artists and decided to send them back home. Surprisingly, our fishing fleet was still allowed to go out and keep fishing until the summer of 1944. A fishing boat could have been used for an escape, but I was not aware of such attempts by an individual. Fast allied MTBs (motor torpedo boats) were occasionally cruising off our coast and were more suitable for organized transport of members of the resistance, who could be picked up or landed at night with a rubber boat.

Still undecided, I went home to stay with my parents for a couple of weeks and work at a local farm, Rust en Vreugd, where I cleaned milk bottles and pleased my parents with a daily bottle of real milk. A letter arrived from the management of the Stoomvaart Maatschappÿ Nederland in Amsterdam (the Nederland Line) with an opening in their training program for apprentice mates and another Ausweis.

The invitation by the Nederland Line in Amsterdam to enrol in their training program was a surprise. I had been under the impression that the administration of the company had effectively ceased to exist with the hasty departure of its two last vessels to leave Amsterdam before the capitulation on May 13th, 1940. The two ships, the *Sembilan* and *Johan de Witt* managed to dodge bombing and strafing by the Luftwaffe throughout their voyage to England. Numerous magnetic mines parachuted by German aircraft near IJmuiden had no effect on their passage because both vessels were equipped with degaussing cables to demagnetize their steel hulls. A third vessel, the liner *Jan Pieterszoon Coen* was towed by the Nederland tugboat *Atjeh* to IJmuiden and scuttled by the Dutch navy to block the fairway to Amsterdam. The Atjeh then headed to England with a contingent of navy personnel on board and on her way picked up forty Jewish refugees who were drifting around in a lifeboat. A post-war publication documenting these events made no mention of Nederland personnel embarking on the departing ships, but they took on Jewish families desperate to get out the country. The Nederland people left behind went to work on a variety of projects such as the training of graduates of nautical and engineering schools, a sort of post-graduate school on the grounds of the Nederland. The German authorities apparently went along with this idea and even provided Ausweises for the "post-grad" students and their teachers.

From the point of view of the organizers, the school would not only help the participants to again "legally" avoid the Arbeitseinsatz, but also provide the company with trained personnel after the war, when many ships' crews would go on extended leave or retire. But why did the Germans support the idea? Who were they? Members of the Kriegsmarine who figured that they could recruit from the school? As far as we knew, they did not. What also puzzled me was that I had been accepted for this training program. My exam marks at the KvdZ were good, but not outstanding. My father, who had always been closely associated with the Nederland, assured me that he had not tried to recommend me and I didn't think that he would. However, it occurred to me that my selection might have been a quiet gesture of respect for my brother Frits, who was out there somewhere in the Atlantic or Pacific as a chief officer in one of the allied convoys.

To make real seamen out of us, the brand-new training school acquired two ocean-going sailboats, the *Holland* and the *Douwes* – about forty feet long would be my guess. The *Holland* was skippered by Mr. Nieboer, the *Douwes* by Mr. van der Worm. Both were deck officers who had been stranded in Amsterdam by the war. Together with four other apprentices, I embarked on the *Holland* under Mr. Nieboer on the 22nd of July, 1944. We were all graduates from nautical schools and in peace time would have embarked on vessels of the Nederland Line as apprentices or *leerlingen*. An apprentice would have to serve at sea for a least one year before going back to school for his third-mate diploma. Traditionally, *leerlingen* were the butt of many jokes by the ship's crew, but we started our training on a sailboat and missed that humiliation.

Our sailing trips on the IJsselmeer ("meer," in Dutch, means "lake") lasted about one week at a time and differed from my sailing in Friesland in that the IJsselmeer was still very much an inland sea, wide open to strong winds from any direction. I was sea sick a couple of times – part of the training! The salinity of the IJsselmeer had been almost completely reduced to zero by the inflow of rivers and creeks entering from the east and south, and by the large dam (the Afsluitdijk) separating it from the North Sea. The lake teemed with a small species of eel that we caught daily with a net and had for dinner, cooked or fried or even smoked in a shack near Volendam. Volendam, where we tied up often if we didn't anchor outside, is a friendly, strongly Catholic community, well known to foreign tourists for its traditional dress.

Air activity above us never seemed to let up during our cruises. We had a bit of a scare one day when a R.A.F. fighter passed over us, then turned around as if to have another look at the *Holland*. We quickly dug up a large Dutch flag and frantically waved it at the aircraft. The pilot made one more pass, then tipped his wings and disappeared. The fishing fleet of Volendam was called in on September 4th because of the air attacks and the *Holland* and the *Douwes* returned to Amsterdam on the 16th of September, having cleared a last check of our Ausweises by the SS on the Oranje locks. I had no problem getting home on one of the evening trains from Amsterdam to Leiden and the streetcar from Leiden to Wassenaar because of the darkness in which the allied fighters did not see their targets. However, at the end of the previous trip with the *Holland*, I'd had to walk three hours from Leiden to Wassenaar.

On September 18th, a general railway strike of the entire network in the Netherlands took effect, and there were no more trips with the *Holland* and the *Douwes*. Both boats were de-rigged and hidden near a lake east of Amsterdam.

With KvdZ

8

THE HUNGER WINTER

Prelude: The Police

The regular (pre-war) police officers in our cities and villages had a tough time doing their job without getting into trouble with either the Dutch Nazis or the anti-Nazis. There was crime everywhere and every day. Newspapers reported raids on banks and distribution centres of food and clothing vouchers without any comments. We knew that these raids were mostly carried out by the Resistance to help the railway strikers, but also by common criminals to help themselves. Even jails were attacked to free arrested members of the underground. Many of the regular police officers were not sympathetic to the Nazis; some of them were even part of the Resistance or hiding Jews in their houses. One of the few legal matters that they did not have to concern themselves with any more was traffic. A year or so after the German invasion, there were hardly any cars on the road. The ones still around usually towed a wood generator to make fuel, or had a big balloon of light gas on top, or were pulled by a horse – even some military German cars. The regular police was normally not involved in *razzias*. *Razzias* were conducted by the Grüne Polizei (dark green uniform) who also looked after the confiscation of hidden radios, the arrest of the radio owners and the *onderduikers*, men hiding from the Arbeitseinsatz ("duiken" meaning "to dive").

There were some auxiliary police detachments recruited from Nazi volunteers. The most hated and despised police corps was the Landwacht (Country Guard) recruited from the Dutch Nazi party, the NSB. Even their German masters did not trust them with regular weapons, but allowed them to carry a shotgun instead of side arms. We sarcastically called them Jan Hagel, John Buckshot. Their uniforms were a sinister black. They helped the Grüne Polizei search houses for radios, Jews or people without an Ausweis.

Then there was the more idealistic SS Freiwilligen Panzergrenadier Brigade "Nederland" of about 20,000 Dutch volunteers who fought with the German SS on the Eastern Front and lost 5,000 men in Russia. A couple of years after the war, some of these Dutch SS survivors were given a chance to redeem themselves by the Dutch government by immigrating to New Guinea in the then Dutch Indies and developing a homestead while basically living in exile. I happened to serve as a third mate on a Nederland freighter carrying eight of these banished men. While on the 8:00 to 12:00 watch in the Indian Ocean, I was asked by the captain to show this group the bridge and talk about my work. The captain had served with the allies in convoys during the war and had little idea about our feelings towards the Nazis, even though he must have spent some time with his family when he returned to Holland after five years on convoy duty, like my brother Frits. I said no to his request. He looked puzzled and told me that they were our passengers and deserved some attention. When I stuck to my refusal, he told me to get the second mate to come to the bridge and host the passengers. I did. The second's reaction? "No way!" The fourth mate, if I remember this well, had been with the Resistance, hiding downed allied flyers in his and his girlfriend's houseboat near Leiden. He was resting on his bunk and stared at me in disbelief. "God-verdomme, Ages, ben je van je lotje getikt?" ("Are you off your rocker?") Back to the

bridge went Ages with the message. The old man was baffled by the
reaction of his deck-officers and did the P.R. job himself. I don't
know how these exiles fared in the jungle of New Guinea, but they
certainly had not chosen a very enviable way of life.

The Dutch volunteer SS brigade was commanded by a general
Seyffardt, a Nazi. He had retired earlier from the Dutch army and
lived with his wife in Voorschoten, a small village a few kilometres
east of our house. During the evening of February 5th, 1943, Johan
Huibregtse came racing over on his bicycle with the message that
I should leave immediately because I was going to be picked up by
the German police that same evening. Seyffardt had been shot dead
by two masked men in his house. His wife had apparently lived to
tell the police that they sounded like juveniles. The German police
had entered the town hall in Wassenaar with one of the municipal
administrators to select twenty young men to be taken hostage.
The administrator had apparently managed to copy the names of
the twenty men, including Johan and me. Johan took off to warn
some other boys and to go into hiding himself. The streetcars were
still running so I grabbed some clothes and set out to The Hague to
spend a night in my aunt Rens' attic or whatever. My father insisted
on going with me and returned with the last streetcar before midnight. When I arrived safely at Tante Rens' place, there were two
other guys hiding in her attic too. It was a safe place to hide. Tante
Rens had a sort of bed and board, mostly for older or single women.
She had survived a couple of search parties who had left totally
frustrated trying to communicate with her because not only didn't
she speak German, but she was partly deaf and spoke Frisian much
better than Dutch. Then the search party had to confront some
old women upstairs, altogether too time consuming for the Grünen
and an interpreter. That night, the three of us just barely fitted in a
big bed and didn't get much sleep because of all the stories we had
to tell one another.

I don't remember if my father fetched me the next day when
the coast was clear, but I was home the next day. My parents had
had quite a night. A German officer (apparently Grüne Polizei
again), accompanied by a Dutch (regular, not Nazi) policeman and

a Landwacht member, arrived well after midnight. Mam told my father to go to the bathroom and stay out of sight while she met the visitors. They wandered all over the house. The Dutch regular policeman stressed that the whole thing was not his idea and that he had nothing to do with the house searches. The Landwacht guy, according to Mam, was a disgusting lickspittle (*Strooplikker* in Dutch), trying to impress the German officer in every way. They felt my bed and under the bed. They didn't take anything. A rifle used by the Boers in their war against the English some forty years ago, which had been on the wall in my room, had already been taken during a previous surprise search. My diaries and pamphlets were well hidden. The German officer opened the door of the bathroom, noticed my naked father in the tub humming some opera to himself and telling the German that "das Wasser ist gerade zu kalt" ("the water is pretty cold"). Obviously embarrassed, the German officer quickly closed the door saying, "Bitte Verzeihung" ("sorry"), and that was the end of the visit. My mother noticed that the German completely ignored the Landwachter but treated the Dutch police-man with respect.

Later I heard that only one of the targeted young men was captured because he had ignored the warning. He was sent to Germany and returned after the war. The house searches coincided with a much larger hunt for sons of "plutocrats" in North and South Holland.

Not much was known about the role of the Resistance in sup-porting the railway strike ordered by the Dutch government in London. One might assume that the frequent bank robberies and raids on distribution centres of food coupons were arranged by the Resistance to help the strikers and their families with money and food. These attacks were treated by both the Nazi and underground presses as routine events, together with the almost daily reports of the elimination of Dutch Nazis and the resulting counter measures by the Nazi regime.

I did not ask brother Nap for details of these raids. He prob-ably knew about the Resistance's efforts to keep the strike alive, but he wouldn't have told his kid brother. Nap was deeply involved

in the Resistance, as an editor of the underground newspaper in
The Hague, *Het Parool*, which was also published in Amsterdam.
This Amsterdam edition still exists under the same name. Nap
was under surveillance by the Gestapo or *Geheime Staats Polizei*,
the secret German police. As a contributor of a well-known and
well-informed aviation magazine, the *Vliegwereld*, which was still
allowed to be published in Holland, Nap had written an article with
technical data which he could only have obtained from a recent
English source; the Gestapo became suspicious. They raided his
"Cheese Export" office that he occupied and advertised. For a journalist, Nap must have been as much at home in the cheese business
as a baseball player in a hockey rink, but he needed this company to
disguise his involvement with the Resistance.

One of the Gestapo intruders happened to be Osendarp, the
famous Dutch medal winner in track and field during the Olympics
in Berlin in 1936. Osendarp was one of the several foreign athletes
lured into Nazism by Hitler's protégée, Leni Riefenstahl. Osendarp
should have continued running around a field as a track star rather
than join the Gestapo slime…. During the Gestapo visit, Nap, who
had been a young journalist in 1936, with his usual flair reminisced
with Osendarp about the Berlin Olympics while the other Gestapo
visitors politely listened. In the meantime, his secretary managed to
stuff the proof copies of *Het Parool's* newest edition into her bosom.
Nobody seemed to notice and the group left empty-handed. Did
perhaps Osendarp notice? We'll never know.

Another Ages, nephew Dirk Ages, had been less fortunate,
becoming the victim of an arbitrary arrest. One day in May 1943,
Dirk was reading a poster on a bill board in The Hague. It warned
against picking up so-called "terror pencils" loaded with explosives
and dropped by the R.A.F. He made a sarcastic remark to a gentleman behind him, who then showed his Gestapo badge. Dirk was
arrested as a "danger to the Reich" and was sent to Silezien to work
in a mine. Dirk might have given the German an earful leading
to his arrest, but it seemed to be a typical example of a martinet
German official trying to impress his Gestapo boss.

As for terror pencils and toys loaded with explosives, nobody I knew ever came across these strange objects. However, I once did run into a more sophisticated gimmick when I was haying in a field near Grouw, Friesland. I picked up a little square platelet, about two inches by two inches, which was lying in a ditch, covered with water. While I was holding it, the platelet started to smoke and heat up. My hands started to smoke and, when I swept my hair out of my face, my hair started to smoke! There were no flames, but I pushed the platelet back under the water. As I later found out, it was a *brand plaatje* or, roughly translated, a "fire platelet" dropped by the R.A.F. at night and the phosphor in the centre would burn when the sun had evaporated the thin layer of water. The pilot might have gotten rid of it with other leftovers on his flight home. I didn't remember what I did with it apart from throwing it in the water. My own "in the field" experience in this particular case differed from the patriotic rumour mill suggesting that the *brand plaatjes* were actually negatives of the Dutch Royal Family in Ottawa and not carriers of phosphor as cautioned by the Nazis for whatever reason. Pictures of our royal princesses were big business among teenagers, but after my experience in Friesland I became a bit cagey with the youthful entrepreneurs.

Nap sometimes brought us a box of butter after a raid of a Nazi farm by the Resistance, for the benefit of the railway strikers and their families. It was just a little bit of butter, of course, but enough to make his parents and young brother happy for a day. Nap took great risks in his work for the Resistance. Once in a while, I cycled to The Hague to visit him, keeping my eyes on the road ahead to avoid German check-points. When I arrived at his house in the centre of The Hague, I could hear his printer in the basement from outside the front door. It probably ran on a few hours a day of electricity allowed in the city. What puzzled me was that the father of his wife, Wil, had been a member of the Dutch Nazi party, the NSB, before the war. He'd left the party out of disgust with its support of the German invasion, but obviously he did not accidentally reveal the underground activities of his son-in-law to some of his former Nazi friends because Nap never got caught.

Wil, Nap's very attractive former secretary with the KLM, was not interested in the Resistance, but his neighbour's wife, Welmoet, was very much involved. She was the daughter of a general in the Dutch army and had a brother, a doctor, who had been arrested early on in the war and survived a concentration camp in Germany. I think it was the notorious camp at Dachau. Welmoet was married to a lawyer who, like Wil, did not share Nap's and Welmoet's patriotic feelings. After the liberation of Holland, the foursome traded partners. Nap and Welmoet had a baby boy named after me, Alard Jan.

Visiting Nap's place was not without some risk. Once, after an overnight stay at his rented house in The Hague, there was an early morning *razzia* in the streets to catch young men for the Arbeitseinatz. My Ausweis then was not valid any more. The German police and military went from house to house. I was having breakfast behind the front windows when I suddenly faced a German looking in.

I didn't wait for the bell to ring. I dropped my plate and ran upstairs, three floors up, went through the window in the attic, jumped from roof to roof and then down on a balcony where I surprised a woman behind the glass door, who screamed. She was in her nightie and just getting dressed. I climbed back onto the roof and jumped down onto the next balcony to hide behind a large barrel until I heard Nap's whistle and worked my way back. The Germans had caught several men, but the one who spotted me through the window had not bothered to ring the bell.

Apart from the discomfort and tremendous logistics of housing and feeding the families of the striking railway workers, the national strike must have been a godsend for the railway personnel and their families. Before the strike, not a day went by without trains being shot up by roving British or American fighters anywhere in the country, and there were many casualties among the train crews, passengers and the personnel who had to look after the junctions and crossings. When I commuted to Amsterdam and had to travel in daylight, I never boarded a train in one of the forward sections because the locomotives were prime targets. Some Spitfire pilots had the decency to make a pass at the train before the fusillade to give the driver a chance to stop and let the passengers run into the field. The fighter pilots had time to be merciful because they did not have to worry about an attack by a German aircraft. The R.A.F. and US Airforce owned the airspace over Holland, having turned the tables on the Luftwaffe. Unfortunately, some of the trigger-happy pilots seemed to strafe anything that moved on the street, forcing people to abandon their cycles, carrier bikes or handcarts to take cover in one of the many holes dug along the highway for protection. I cared too much for my bicycle to leave it unattended while taking cover in a hole and sometimes lay down flat on my belly behind a tree. I got a kick out of watching all these heads pop up at the same time from their holes after a couple of Spitfires or Hurricanes had swooped by. Then there were the Typhoons with their noisy rockets to destroy cars and trucks, but they did not stay very long because there were no more vehicles on the road in the daytime after October.

A few years ago, there was a unique show near the airport of Victoria, British Columbia, where some of the military planes used by the allies and the Germans during the war were on display. The aircraft were open to the public. Among the bombers was a Heinkel III, the only one left after the second world war, and now used in movies. The Heinkel III bombed Rotterdam and various other cities

in Europe during the war. One could easily recognize this type by
its strange attitude (a plane's position in the air with respect to its
flight direction), its tail conspicuously below the level of the nose.
I went aboard and slipped into the roped-off cockpit to sit in the
pilot's seat for a while. I wondered how a German pilot must have
felt when he approached Rotterdam. Or Warschau, or Belgrado.
And then my thoughts turned to the R.A.F. Lancasters ordered by
Arthur Harris to set peaceful Dresden on fire. Regardless of their
nationality, the pilots were all volunteers, just like the paratroopers
near Wassenaar in May, 1940.

The V2

On the evening of the 8th of September, 1944, Wassenaarders
were startled by an earsplitting thunder clap somewhere in the
woods south of the town. There had been no warning. People on
the street ran around in panic, looking for shelter or simply lying
face-down anywhere with their hands protecting their heads.
Scared dogs and screaming children frantically tried to get into
their homes. Then, two enormous cigar-shaped bodies followed
by plumes of fire ascended from the wood, straight up for a while
before turning west.

We had heard about the V1s, the "flying bombs" fired by the
Germans across the Channel to London, but this wasn't a V1; it was
much bigger and it did not have little wings like the V1. It had fire
behind it, a rocket, an enormous rocket!

I didn't either see or hear the launching. I was still on my way home
from a sail on the IJsselmeer and had just started my three hours' walk
home from Leiden so I missed the event but not the graphic stories of
my parents and neighbours. The shocked citizens of Wassenaar had
just witnessed the launching of the first V2 from occupied Europe to
England, as if this quiet town had not been shaken enough by the landing of the Fallschirmjäger a few years earlier and then by the arrival
of the top German brass to confiscate its luxurious villas, thereby

drawing the relentless attention of the allied fighter pilots.

According to the Nazi propaganda, the "V" stands for *Vergeltung*: retaliation. My father, who had supervised the design of German ships' engines for the Nederland Line, told me that in the German ship building and aeronautical industry, "V" (Vau in German) means *Versuch*: trial. The V1 was deployed first: an unmanned, rather small jet plane with explosives in the nose. The plane ("flying bomb") went as far as the fuel would last. What was scary about this ugly little monster was that when the "put put put" throbbing of its motor overhead suddenly stopped, it would be out of fuel, crash and explode on impact. The V2 struck without warning and blew up. They could not be directed to a small target. Both models were designed and tested in Peenemünde on the shore of the Baltic near the Polish boundary and built underground in the Harz mountains in Germany.

A couple of years before the outbreak of the war in 1939, my parents took me along to the Harz on their vacation. We spent a couple of weeks in the small village of Elend. On our way in a German train, we shared a compartment with two German boys of my age (13), in a brown uniform with swastikas. They glanced at me with some disdain, perhaps because I wasn't wearing the same uniform. When they realized that I was not German, they became a little more pleasant.

The Harz is a lone mountain range in the vast northern German plains. It is about one hundred and eighty kilometres long and thirty wide. Its highest mountain, the Brocken, rises to one thousand, one hundred and forty-two metres above sea level. The mountains attract relatively few tourists, which surely was why my parents picked the Harz for their rare vacation. The German poet Goethe sometimes spent part of the winter in the Harz, probably for the same reason. We stayed in a small hotel in Elend and spent most of our time hiking in the mountains, visiting with a shepherd and his bell-carrying cattle, and went up the Brocken, a treeless, windy summit. We also descended a few times into the very large caves, where I learned about stalactites and stalagmites and about fish that were blind because there was no light in the caverns.

Of course, we had no idea about what would be going on in the
innards of these peaceful mountains a few years later when thirty
thousand forced labourers detained by the Germans in France,
Holland and Eastern Europe were herded down into a huge underground factory to construct V1 and V2 terror weapons. Thirty-two
thousand V1s and fourteen thousand V2s were built here in 1943
and 1944. I wonder if these wretched prisoners succeeded in sabo-
taging some rockets, judging from the misfires and accidents at the
sites near Wassenaar.

One of the less known differences in the design of the two V
models was the starting procedure. The V1 was launched from
a long, slightly tilted track which could be detected from the air;
the V2 started from a small pad on a stable subsoil such as sand
or even an asphalt street. Wassenaar was chosen by the Germans
as a base for storing and launching the V2 because it was the only
coastal site along the southern coast of Holland with a wooded
area of large trees to hide the fourteen-metre-long V2 before being
launched from a standing position. Moreover, the rockets could
be transported from Germany to Leiden at night and from there to
Wassenaar by large trucks (so-called Meiller trucks) specially built
for the V2s. The convoy did not always follow the same nightly
route from Leiden to the site in Wassenaar, but at times, when the
moon was out, I could see the three trucks quietly sneak through our
street, the first one with men, then the enormous rocket strapped

to the Meiller truck and the third vehicle, a tank truck loaded with the propellant, liquid oxygen and methyl alcohol as I later found out. I did not see any camouflage on the V2, or a tarp. The body clearly reflected the moonlight and would have been an easy target for R.A.F. night fighters if they had bothered to show up. The V2 would reach the site before day break to be stored and prepared for one of the next liftoffs, when the long body was turned upright by the Meiller's gear, its four stabilizing rocket fins resting on the pad. After fuelling, an officer applied a torch to the gas turbine and up it went, rising about one hundred kilometres, then travelling west to crash somewhere in London with a ton of explosives, five minutes after blastoff.

Nowadays, the liftoff of a rocket or a spaceship can be watched on TV almost daily, but the launching of the first V2s more than sixty years ago was an event that no old-timer from Wassenaar will ever forget. Some enterprising and gutsy villagers risked their freedom and even their lives trying to elude the German guards and sneak through the nearby bushes to get a closer look at the huge projectiles, or even better, at their actual liftoff. I did not think it was worth the risk of getting caught and going on another trip to the Harz, this time not as a tourist wandering in its woods but as a prisoner assembling rockets in its caves.

The thunder during the first V2 launch, which had led to such a panic in Wassenaar, had become the order of the day, even among the children. Nobody paid attention to it any more. What also became the order of the day was a misfire. We could tell that something had gone awry in those woods when, a few seconds after the start of the distant rumble, all went quiet, at times followed by one or two loud explosions (fuel and/or warhead), meaning that the rocket had lifted off the pad and fallen back again. Or, if the rumble stopped after a couple of seconds and there were no explosions, the V2 was still on the pad and anything might happen. The worst disaster occurred on October 27th, 1944, when a V2 fell down at the site from a height of ninety metres and killed twelve Germans. Several ambulances raced by our house after the explosion, so we could only guess what had happened.

Some people counted to eighty after a liftoff and if the noise hadn't suddenly stopped, all would be well because the V2 had passed our coastline and was above the North Sea. One day I noticed a V2 going east instead of west after it had climbed one hundred metres and moved into its horizontal trajectory. Maybe it was homesick! Another entry in my diary might be more pertinent to meteorology than to the design problems of the V2. On November 11th, 1944, a number of conspicuous black lines briefly appeared in the blue sky ahead of a V2 moving West. The black lines looked like a series of tangents progressively following an imaginary curve and stretching all over the firmament. This phenomenon occurred only once during my observations.

It didn't take long before the roaming Spitfires found the V2 base. Less than a week after the first dramatic V2 launch, a couple of Spitfires happened to fly in from the North Sea when they spotted a V2 about to rise from its pad. They immediately moved in and destroyed the rocket with their two centimetre cannons. From then on, it was open season on V2 bashing. The first wave of seventeen, four-engine Lancasters arrived four days later. The leading aircraft, the "pathfinder," dropped his *Kerst boompje* (Dutch for "little Christmas tree" – a cluster of lights lowered to guide the following planes) to lead their runs, carpet bombing the site (covering an area rather than aiming at a single target). My mother and Stien took cover under our staircase; my father wasn't home. I opened our windows to prevent damage by the blasts caused more by suction than pressure from a bomb explosion. I lay down in the yard, flat on my back – I suffer from claustrophobia in any kind of air-raid shelter – and watched the large bombers starting their dive just about right over our street. The raid took less than half an hour and was followed by a couple of Thunderbolt fighters, probably to take pictures of the damage. There were more similar raids later on. I was not impressed by this method of carpet bombing; shortly after the raid, another V2 went up.

Mishaps

I sometimes wondered how, after a long flight across the North Sea, these little Spitfires could sustain their harassment of the V2 sites and other targets without running out of fuel. The ten-year-old boy next door enlightened me. He was one of the kids who collected all kinds of war stuff and had become an expert in disassembling misfired grenades and other debris jettisoned by overflying planes. He picked up a detachable gas tank dropped by one of the fighters while strafing traffic on the highway between Wassenaar and The Hague. Fritsje Jol took it to the garage outside the house. The tank still contained some gas. Fritsje threw a match in it and blew up the garage. He died in the hospital the next day, October 7th, 1944. Frits was a cool kid and his father, a dentist, was of course devastated, but he could not always be home to check on his enterprising youngest son.

The whole Jol family had been forced by the Germans to evacuate from Scheveningen to our village further inland. Our previous neighbour, a minister, Dr. Nauta, had had to leave to make room for the Jols – a rather strange arrangement possibly based on family size and dwelling space. Although Dr. Nauta was a good man, I didn't object to this change of neighbours since one of the girls in the Jol family played guitar to accompany my mandolin; we had some great sessions in spite of all the war noise around us.

My father, who was totally a-musical, had a lot of patience with his family. He was teaching ship's engineers privately in his own room upstairs, one or two at a time, to prepare them for exams when, some day, the war would be over. On the same floor, there I was playing string instruments in my room with the girl next door while below his room, my mother prepared a choir of fifteen local girls for a Christmas performance. The odd Spitfire overhead looking for German traffic on the nearby highway added to the noise. We were lucky to be allowed to continue living in our house, possibly due to my parents needing the space for teaching and having the qualifications to do so, each in their own field. My mother wasn't involved in choirs all year, of course; she also taught string instruments (violin, guitar). She had traded her grand piano for food, mainly meat, at a local farm. Farmers preferred goods to money.

Young Fritsje's fatal accident with the Spitfire's jettisoned fuel tank was engraved in my mind, in particular when, a couple of months after his tragic death, a projectile whistled past me in our yard during a sortie of Spitfires overhead. I noticed a small hole in the ground and carefully dug down until the shovel touched metal. I put a sign in the ground in Dutch ("Blindganger") and English ("Grenade"). I then went into the house and went to bed, not saying anything to my parents. I couldn't sleep and got up at daybreak, put my heavy gloves on and starting digging around the object. There was my mother, always up early.

"Wat doe je, Alard?"

"Nieuw boompje, Mam, voor jou, voor kerstmis. Kijk niet!" (A new little tree, mom, for you, for Christmas. Don't look!")

I put some dirt in the hole and waited till my nosy and concerned parents had left for a while. With a long-handled spoon and heavy leather gloves, I finally extricated a two centimetre-diameter grenade (as was used by the Spitfires against armoured vehicles) inch by inch from the soil, lifted it onto a shovel on the ground and carried it to the foot of a large stump in the back of our yard. Then, lying flat on my belly, protected by the stump, I unscrewed the head of the grenade with two long-handled pliers. It came off! After shaking the powder out of the now-harmless case, I had a closer look at the little grenade and found out why it had not exploded in my face: the pin resting against the tiny percussion cap in the head was dislodged a fraction of a millimetre. One little shake of the projectile and it would have blasted my hand off. I'd never do this again.

I confessed to my parents when they came home later in the day. My mother had a fit; my father did not say anything. I was very lucky. Some others, like Fritsje Jol, were not. The girl with whom I sometimes worked in the milk factory capping milk bottles got killed when she ran into a minefield to save her dog. The dog made it out. A herd of forty cows strolled through another minefield near Wassenaar and all animals survived. I read in the newspaper that, in The Hague, two sisters, Emmy and Annie Dorst, were killed in February, 1944 by another jettisoned fuel tank when the tank fell through the roof of their house and onto a burning stove, trapping one of the teenage girls while the other one tried to jump out of the window and also died.

As the war seemed to approach its climax with the advance of allied troops in Belgium and the southern provinces of the Netherlands, there were sudden outbursts of joy throughout the country, culminating in the *Dolle Dinsdag* (Crazy Tuesday), a rather premature celebration of freedom of North and South Holland. Thousands of people lined up along the highways and streets with flags and decorations to welcome the liberating allied troops. Many well-known Dutch Nazis left Wassenaar in a hurry, moving east to Germany. Nobody had the faintest idea where this massive demonstration originated, but the allies were still south of the large rivers Waal, Maas and Rhine, nowhere near the provinces forming actual Holland. Before Christmas, the American army was about to face a determined and well-equipped German army in the Belgian Ardennes. They suffered heavy losses, although they prevented the Germans from breaking out to the vital harbour of Antwerpen.

I was at sea at that time, sailing on the IJsselmeer near Volendam and wasn't aware of Dolle Dinsdag at all, except for a strange, almost comical incident in Volendam on that Tuesday. A motor cyclist arrived in the centre of the town. The Volendammers were not familiar with his uniform and promptly welcomed him as an American soldier. He was surrounded with ecstatic Volendammers in their usual traditional costumes and wooden shoes. They showered him with bright orange marigolds and other patriotic adornments. The attention obviously embarrassed him and when some of them tried to speak English, he said that he could speak Dutch. One of the villagers suggested that he must be a uniformed resistance fighter, triggering an approving howl from the crowd. But then some smart kid recognized the little black SS marks on the man's collar and shouted that he was with the Dutch SS – a traitor! A woman screamed that he had a carabine and was about to start shooting, which generated another clattering of wooden shoes, away from the town's square. Apparently, the SS-er had been sent to Volendam to confiscate motorbikes, but he didn't get any and disappeared quickly on his own bike. We heard all about this Volendam version of *Dolle Dinsdag* from the locals after we had tied up in the harbour.

House Bound

What a drag. Any further training cruises on the IJsselmeer had to be cancelled after the railway strike, not only because there were no trains running to Amsterdam anymore, but also in view of the possibility of some trigger-happy allied fighter mistaking our boat for a German yacht.

Having bamboozled a German soldier at a checkpoint in Wassenaar once with an expired Aussweis, I did not want to risk another road check and stayed home during the day most of the time. I busied myself taking the three large poplars down in our yard behind the house. I used a handsaw and a small axe. We would be provided with firewood for at least a few weeks. I also felled my favourite birch near the pond, saving a piece for a candle holder. It still decorates my desk. Several hours a day went to studying music and once in a while I ventured out into the open to visit a friend like Johan Huibregtse in another part of Wassenaar or vice versa. None of us ever got caught. Willem Thijsse lived in The Hague and was hiding at his girlfriend's place. They got married after the war.

I very much missed our dog, Sobat Juul. A couple of years earlier, we were notified by the German authorities that we had to hand over our Great Dane to be trained for "field duty." All dogs in our area over fifty centimetres high were claimed and we knew what this field duty was all about. The big dogs were trained to carry explosives to enemy targets and then to blow up with the target. We did not know where to hide this huge dog; she was too conspicuous to escape detection, even on a farm. When Sobat was to be picked up the next day, my father decided to kill her, rather than hand her over. He called the vet, who came the same evening to euthanize her with my father assisting. I remember lying on my bed in my room above the garage where Sobat had her bed. I heard a brief yelp and knew it was the end. The first thing to come to my mind was to quickly take myself out too; it wouldn't be too difficult, but it wouldn't help Sobat Juul or anybody else. I had been thinking of taking her to a farm in Friesland where she would be safe, but how? There was no transportation and if we walked all the way, it would have taken several weeks and we both would have been caught. Several ideas had come to my mind, but it was too late. All I could do now was put my head in my pillow and cry, and someday get back at the bastards. My parents left me alone until the next day, when I dug a grave in the yard.

The next morning, my father met a German officer at the door. He saluted and said, "Der Hund, bitte."

"Der Hund ist tot," my father replied. "Wollen Sie mal sehen?" (The dog is dead. Would you like to see?)

"Nein, danke," the German said, "das ist nicht nötig, ich begreife es." (No, thank you. I understand.) Then he told my father that he was a vet and never wanted that kind of work.

Sobat Juul had joined us as a seven-month-old pup just before the war. We picked her up at the asiel (Dutch for asylum, the SPCA in Canada). She was a black Great Dane, a very sick dog, but she recuperated quickly from what we thought was a bout of distemper. In those years, we didn't know much about what ailed our dogs or cats. We called her Sobat, and Indonesian word for "friend," and quite common in Holland. The second name, Juul, came later during the war when many people named their dogs after our Royal House. Juul is short for (princess) Juliana. Sobat was so big that she would rest her head on the corner of the dinner table and drool all over the fancy table cloth. I watched in amazement until my mother came in from the kitchen and read the riot act. She lived in our dog kennel a few hours a day and then howled and barked to be let out while I tried to study for my gymnasium exams. I once lost my cool and beat her with a stick in her doghouse. Sobat lost her cool too. She lunged at me unexpectedly, threw me on my back and jumped on top of me, having me at her mercy. She bloodied both hands, but not my face, and then sat down on the grass. I was scared. Then I went over to her and said, "Kom" (Come with me). She let me put her leash on and we went for a brief walk. I told my parents and suggested that she should be in the house and not in a cage. They agreed and from then on my father took her to the nearby race track to run with another big dog, Mirza, and all was well. At least for a few years.

How did the German military know that we had a Great Dane over fifty centimetres high? What made it so difficult for anybody to hide animals and precious property from the Germans was the detailed inventory of the Dutch administration, which fell into the hands of the Germans through the Dutch Nazis. My father had bought the latest model of a Philips radio, just before the German invasion in May, 1940. It was an expensive set, almost a piece of furniture by itself. It even had push buttons to select stations, a gimmick unheard of in 1939. My father had the good foresight to have a friend lift this radio's registration from its files in The Hague almost immediately after the capitulation of the Dutch in May, 1940. The big Philips set became an indispensable piece of furniture throughout the war as long as we had an hour or two of power per day.

With a lack of power in mind, I retrieved the parts of a crystal radio which I had built as a twelve year old explorer before I switched to a much more sophisticated super-heterodyne radio. I rebuilt the crystal radio with its various coils and a "cat's whisker" and had good reception of the news. For those not familiar with this interesting little radio, I might mention that a crystal receiver does not need batteries or any form of electricity. In Holland, it picks up a signal from an AM station as far away as England, provided that we listen to it through earphones and not with a loudspeaker. The cat's whisker is a small piece of wire with which one tickles a small crystal to find the station. The problem in my case was the need of a twenty-metre-long horizontal antenna running from a tree to my window which, of course, would alert a snooping and knowledgeable Nazi.

Immediately after the capitulation, we stopped listening to Radio Hilversum, the Dutch broadcast now under the control of the Nazis. We switched to the BBC on May 16th, 1940, or to the broadcast in Dutch from London, Radio Oranje, on the forty-one and forty-nine metre wavelengths. Throughout the occupation years, I listened almost daily to the BBC in English because it improved my English (with the help of a dictionary) and it was factual and clear. Radio Oranje was too provocative; we didn't need propaganda. After July 7th, 1940, anybody caught listening to the British broadcast was fined, went to jail and their radio was confiscated. All radios throughout the country had to be handed in on May 24th, 1943. We did not, of course. My father and I took our fancy Philips to the attic and stored it behind the wainscot. We did not tell Mam; she'd be too nervous during a house search. As far as she knew, we had handed it in. We still had electricity – at first all day, later a couple of hours a day – until, during the last winter, we had none at all in most streets. Without telling my father, I rigged up an electric wire behind the wainscot from the radio to a receptacle behind a bed, connected the radio and, lying on my belly on the beams, listened to the BBC or Radio Oranje with earphones. Then I told my parents the news which I "picked up at my neighbour's place."

One night, I went back to the little hide-out to listen to the radio and found another wire connected to another receptacle. And the hatch leading to the hide-out was open. I crawled in and suddenly heard the BBC announcer loud and clear.

"THIS IS THE BBC HOME AND FORCES PROGRAM. HERE IS THE NEWS AND IT IS FRANK PHILIPS READING," loud enough to be heard through the roof on the street!

It was my father lying on his belly behind the wainscot under the roof listening without earphones and at high volume because he was a bit deaf. I was furious. I carefully crawled behind him and shouted in German to scare him and make him think that he was caught. "Was machen Sie? Sind Sie verrückt? Sie sind in Haft!" (What are you doing? Are you crazy? You're under arrest!) Father Jelte didn't move for a while, then turned his head and spotted me by the light of the radio. He had a good sense of humour and agreed to let me listen to the news as before with earphones and to go on pretending with everyone else that I was picking up the news at a neighbour's place.

There were other incidents of a similar nature. One of our neighbours went outside after dark and, with his ear against the front window, checked if he could hear his radio, hidden somewhere in his living room. Suddenly, he was hit hard in his behind and fell on his face. His attacker had disappeared when he got up, but the next day a guy told him that he had caught somebody with his ear against my neighbour's front window, listening for a radio. He'd kicked the traitor in his behind so hard he fell on his face. I guess they got it straightened out in the end!

"Plenus venter non studet libenter."

"A full stomach does not study with pleasure."

My father picked up this saying when he took first-year Latin with me at the gymnasium. When I was struggling for the finals at the gymnasium and later at the KvdZ, I sometimes complained to my mother that I needed more food to get better marks. So my father painted the message in Latin on a little board and gave it to me as a birthday present to be hung above my desk. As the dreaded hunger winter came upon us in November, 1944, it wasn't all that funny anymore and when I emigrated to Canada in 1953, I took it with me as a memento of our life during the occupation, together with my guitar and the speed skates.

When reading my diary's comments on the hunger winter, one might get the impression that the increasing success of the German *razzias* in the big cities in South Holland was simply due to the local shortage of food, which would lure some men to even volunteer to work in Germany. According to my notes at that time, some men in Rotterdam were all set to be picked up with their gear when the Germans came to search their houses. A sociologist would have a field day explaining why, in November, 1944, the German police netted fifty thousand men in Rotterdam versus ten thousand in The Hague. Both *razzias* lasted one day. Are Hagenaars smarter?

The November *razzias* actually took place on the 21st of that month and it did not come as a surprise to anyone in Wassenaar when we saw tram after tram travel empty through our village to The Hague. They passed our house at the van Zuylen van Nijevelt straat. One of these southbound trams was occupied by a large group of members of the Luftwaffe, who had become more and more associated with the police work of the Grünen since they had lost most of their fleet over Holland and England in the earlier years of the war and, later, were replaced by the unmanned V1s and V2s. The airmen had to be involved in the German war effort somehow, but they weren't very good police men. Unaware of their new job with the Grünen in the fall of 1944, I was stopped on my bicycle by a young Luftwaffe type in his grey uniform and asked for my Ausweis. It had expired and he knew it.

"Verfallen," he said ("Expired.") and shook his head.

But then he handed it back to me and with a big grin waved me through. So I smiled too and got back on my bike but picked another route on the way back just in case a Grüne had taken over his control post.

Judging from the many grey uniforms in the otherwise empty trams heading for the *razzias* in The Hague, we were not surprised to see the Luftwaffe move from destroying open cities to catching defenceless industrial slaves. From my attic window, I kept an eye on the trams passing through our street to Leiden on their return trip from The Hague. They were packed with men, obviously caught by the *razzia* in that city. In Leiden, the men would be transferred to a night train to continue on, possibly to work camps in Germany. The noise coming from some of these trams was unbelievable. The prisoners were yelling and singing dirty Dutch songs and insulting their German guards as the vehicles passed under my window. When the tram had to slow down for a curve nearby, I noticed some guys jumping out and disappearing in the yards across the streets. Of course, I kept out of sight because I was still hiding, albeit in our own house. I would have preferred to move to a remote farm in Friesland, but the trains were not running anymore and I might lose my bike.

A year earlier, I had watched similar transports of Jews passing in the same trams. The difference in the behaviour of the prisoners was remarkable. The Jews, many with wives and children, were quiet and sombre. There was hardly a sound and no attempt to break away. We didn't know that they were heading for Auschwitz or some other death camp and neither did they. The *razzia* men from The Hague had no idea about their destination either but acted like a bunch of nutheads on their way to a soccer game, just to vent their anger. To a holed-up teenager, watching this crazy spectacle was almost refreshing.

After my runin with the German police (fortunately a broad-minded Luftwaffe conscript), I remained cloistered at home a lot more and never far from the hiding place behind the wainscot. The hiding place didn't just store the radio but also blankets, clothing and some canned food hoarded by Mam. The German police, assisted by the Landwacht, had started searching houses for these items in addition to men hiding from the Arbeitseinsatz. I timed myself to disappear quickly and quietly from the moment the police would come to our front door. I thought sometimes of my buddies in Wassenaar, who quite likely went though the same routine, and of the thousands and thousands of men between eighteen and forty who might not even have the opportunity to wander around the house or in the yard to stretch a little bit because their neighbours were Nazis and would have reported them. Listening to the radio news was out of the question in the last couple months of 1944 because the electricity in our street was cut off most of the time. Neighbours behind us in the next street, the Santhorst Laan, had electricity because that street housed some military Germans; the fuses of the other residents on the Santhorst Laan were pulled and the supposedly empty fuse boxes were checked regularly by a German inspector. This young couple whom I only remember by their first names – Vera and Evert – replaced the plugs whenever they wanted to listen to the BBC news with their well-hidden radio and shared it all with my father. The gutsy couple actually committed three severe offences: still having a radio, listening to the BBC and tapping electricity. But they got away with it. I was almost certain that they had made a deal with the inspector, which wasn't all that uncommon, although we never discussed it. They must also have instructed their four-year-old daughter very strongly never to talk about it to anybody. Obviously she didn't; a very wise little girl.

The mere suggestion of making a deal with a German inspector to tamper with the readings on a circuit board would have been unthinkable a few years earlier. Corruption and decay started to infiltrate the disillusioned German military. The entertaining sight of singing German troops marching through our streets had ceased. According to my diary notes, the soldiers seemed to get into trouble with their officers. I had the impression that some of these men started to sing out of tune or out of time deliberately. Indeed, there was a sudden order to halt, stand still for awhile and listen to the officer's sermon. The officers became so frustrated that they gathered their men in a garden or large room in a requisitioned villa to take singing lessons, much to the amusement of passersby and neighbours. A weird nation, those Germans. There they are, marching along in a foreign and hostile street, with armadas of flying fortresses on their way to Hamburg or Bremen, and they have to concentrate on singing in tune.

"Heimat, deine Sterne, der Himmel ist wie ein Diamant!" ("My Fatherland, the heaven is like a diamond," one of their favourites.)

Apart from the disappearance of vehicles from our streets and hence of traffic rules and stop signs, most of the Nazis had also taken off to the Eastern provinces and Germany. We could discuss politics with a stranger without having to worry that we'd be talking to a member of the Gestapo. They were likely the first ones to move East.

Most books and documentaries on the Hunger Winter seem to focus on North and South Holland, where millions of families are crammed into apartment buildings and housing complexes in the big cities of Amsterdam, The Hague and Rotterdam. Indeed, the northernmost provinces of Friesland and Groningen were less affected by any serious food shortage compared with the big cities that made up our original Holland. While staying on the farm in Grouw, Friesland, during the first years of the occupation, I hardly noticed that there was a war on, and Groningen wasn't any different. In fact, my parents kept receiving *Liebesgaben* (gifts of love) from our friend Doddie in the city of Groningen, mostly peas and wheat. Doddie used to live with her mother, Theodora, across our street in Wassenaar well before the war. She studied in Leiden and ended up as a biology professor at the University of Groningen. Her mother put my father's hat on a peg in her vestibule to discourage the gypsies from forcing their way through the front door. As for those gypsies, when I was a bad boy, my mother threatened to hand me to gypsies. I once spotted a gypsy woman walk through our gate to sell pencils; I ran upstairs and hid in the attic. The gypsies lived in a nearby caravan. Most of them were killed by the Germans during the war in Poland (1939).

Well before and during the winter, we received *liebesgaben* from our Swiss friends in Winterthur, the Wyss family, with whom my parents and brothers had stayed for about a year during my father's work with Sulzer, before I was born. The Wyss family kept sending us all kinds of food and even Turkish cigarettes for my father. They were incredible, and we sometimes wondered if they realized how much these gifts meant to us. I also must give a lot of credit to the mail service, which never seemed to fail, although a package mailed in Groningen took about as much time to reach us as one from Switzerland (two weeks). The *Liebesgaben* were not opened or tampered with. The mail went through, even during the railway strike when the mail service at times had to use a small barge pulled by a horse through the canals – a remarkable achievement. We also received telegrams from brother Frits when his vessel called at a neutral port like Beira before joining a convoy.

Once a week, our girl Stien took me to her home in the village to eat potatoes. Her father had a potato patch at their house near the centre of Wassenaar. Stien and her older sister, Cor Noordover, lived in their very old and charming little house which, a couple of years ago, was declared a heritage house. Cor, now well into her nineties, is the only living member of the family and we still correspond once a year. One night per week, I ventured out in the evening on my bike with a screened head lamp to smuggle a couple litres of milk from the nearby farm. The container was flat and slightly bent to follow the shape of my belly so I could hide the milk in case the Landwacht stopped me – a remote possibility because they were easy targets, not so much for our resistance as for any amateur sniper, in particular since nobody would worry about any German countermeasures when it came to the Landwacht.

And then there was our tobacco tragedy. My father had started a miniature tobacco plantation covering most of our backyard. It was his first try and he had endless conversations with some of his knowledgeable buddies in our neighbourhood who were also doing similar research projects. Of course, tobacco products had disappeared from any shops for years, which didn't bother me at all because I had a wager with father Jelte that I wouldn't smoke until I was nineteen years old (I won). Father Jelte and his tobacco patch were inseparable and he was all set to harvest and start the curing process when I went to the backyard and found my father totally devastated.

"All gone," he managed to stammer. "Stolen. De schurken!" (This was a very derogatory word in Dutch; there is no similar expression in English, not even in Canadian English.)

What seemed to upset him even more was that my mother did not commiserate with him. I'm sure she had nothing to do with it, but she didn't seem to be surprised that someone had taken off with the product of my father's efforts. I don't know how my father's friends fared with this enterprise. Perhaps they were also victimized because nobody talked of tobacco anymore.

So what did we eat?

The former premier of British Columbia, Willem van der Zalm, a colourful immigrant from Holland, once told an audience that, during the Hunger Winter, many Dutch households had tulip bulbs instead of potatoes for dinner. The audience's reaction was skeptical, but he was right, we did. And he should know because his flourishing business in the rich loam fields behind the dunes west of Leiden was growing bulbs. He should perhaps have mentioned that tulips were the only edible bulbs and we were warned that other flower bulbs like hyacinths and narcissi were unsafe.

During the first week of December, the food distribution allowed each person to purchase, every two weeks, the following: two kilograms of bread, one hundred and forty grams of meat, one hundred grams of cheese, one hundred and fifty grams of jam, sugar or syrup, and two kilograms of potatoes. These groceries went to households that did not receive their meals from the community kitchen.

My diary does not list the prices of the legally purchased food, but it does show some black market prices rated against the cost of a train ticket, which was F 1.25 for a typical fifty-kilometre railway section from Amsterdam to Leiden, via Haarlem. F stands for Florin, a Dutch guilder. I used the cost of a ticket for a commonly used railway section to give some idea of the black market prices because train tickets did not fluctuate with demand – even if the train stopped running for a while.

Some black market prices in Florins for December 1944:

1 lb butter – F 27
1 egg – F 1.50
1 kg meat – F 25
1 kg sugar – F 15
1 L milk – F 1
1 apple – F 0.40
1 rabbit – F 30
1 pair of shoes – F 80
1 oz tea – F 75
1 glass of Jenever gin – F 0.60; second glass – F 2.50

Compare that to a fifty kilometre train trip for F 1.25.

Four years earlier, the price of Jenever had gone into a tailspin in the village of Noordwijk north of Wassenaar when two barrels of gin floated ashore on the 10th of December, creating some days of great merriment in this otherwise so serene community.

Perhaps the most sinister consequence of the nationwide *razzias* to catch men between the ages of sixteen and fifty for the Arbeitseinsatz was the hunger journey. Thousands of women, old men and children, set out from the big cities into the country with handcarts, wheelbarrows and even bicycles without tires to search for food. Money did not mean much anymore to the farmers; they traded their goods for whatever their hungry visitors had to offer: clothing, ornaments, gold, silver. And then the city people had to wheel their much heavier purchases all the way back to the city. Few of the women and the mostly elderly men were used to this kind of labour and there were casualties. Young men like myself and my friends, in the prime of our lives, had to stay home and watch this caravan from a safe distance.

Our age group wouldn't have lasted very long on the road. On our way back with a landcart filled with potatoes, wheat and other goodies, we would have been stopped by the Grünen or Landwacht at the outskirts of our town, deprived of our hard-earned food and sent of to a labour camp in Germany. I was not aware of anyone being caught this way because we had smartened up and let our sisters and girlfriends and grandfathers become the family providers. As far as I know, and I must say this for the Germans, women were seldom asked for their identification or otherwise harassed. I knew of a young man dressing like a girl, with lipstick and a wig, walking arm and arm with two real girls, doing all the talking at a check point, and getting away with it. Another guy was not so lucky. He also dressed up like a girl and tried to cycle past a check point on a girl's bicycle. He had had to get off his bike for a moment, probably while waiting for someone else being checked through, but when he tried to get on again, he lifted his leg over the saddle instead of in front of it. His skirt became tangled up and the poor man fell off and was caught.

Apart from the food parcels sent by concerned friends and relatives outside the beleaguered western provinces, there were some really moving local acts of compassion such as road signs on farms and stores reading "Hier Kunnen tien Kinderen gratis eten." (Ten children are welcome here for a free dinner.) Even the authorities became involved. On October 18th, 1944, the mayor of near-starving Amsterdam called upon its citizens to help harvest potatoes in the Eastern province of Drente for four weeks. Transportation by barge had been arranged and the Reichs Kommissar Seiss Inquart had formally promised not to have any of the workers detained for other purposes.

An interesting improvement in food quality came about in our family's bread since wheat could no longer be transported after the railway strike. We did not buy bread from the community kitchens; my mother baked bread with ingredients she somehow acquired locally (perhaps with music lessons?).

Often overlooked as one of the most vital parts of our daily food is water. In Wassenaar and other coastal villages, rain water is naturally filtered by the dunes, but after the battle in these dunes between the Dutch troops and the German parachutists in May, 1940, the fallen soldiers had been buried in the dunes, obviously contaminating the water supply. They had to be removed and buried again in their home towns. There seemed to be no problems with the water quality in Wassenaar after the war, but one wonders how the municipal authorities would have coped if the war had lasted much longer.

Mam cooked on our fireplace in the living room. Of course, there was no more electricity, gas or anthracite. We just had to dress warmly and keep feeding the fireplace. There were the innovators who created electricity with a stationary bicycle that they kept pedalling on and on, as if their life depended on it, but I didn't think that they generated more energy than for a four-volt light. Then there were the walking sticks with a little wheel at the bottom end. They were pushed along the pavement to generate a small blue light which would hardly have been effective in the field. The best generator would have been a windmill on top of one's roof. I never noticed any; they were too expensive and could easily be swiped. I preferred the popular Philips hand dynamo, the "Knijpkat" (the Squeezed Cat). Everybody had a Knijpkat. One could hear the whining of its little squeezer all over the street or in the house. After the war, as an apprentice on the first supply ship to the then Dutch East Indies, the *Tarakan*, I bought several dozen Knijpkatten in Amsterdam, expecting to sell them to the locals in Java, where they would then have been a novelty. However, none of the Javanese were impressed because they were quite happy using batteries. Instead of making a quick fortune, I had to sell the whole lot for half price to the crew members of the *Tarakan*.

The large-scale *razzias* in The Hague seemed to have come to an end on the first of December and our baker returned to give Mam a break from baking bread. He had been hiding in The Hague where he had been trapped during the man hunt. He told Mam that he and a friend had been lying flat under the floor of his house for a

week, surfacing only for a meal or to go to the toilet, and just to
stretch. The German police searched the house twice. Their boots
stamping on the floor above them set off clouds of dust in their
hideout and they had difficulty not sneezing. I empathized with
the baker's sneezing peril; it reminded me of a small, bug-infested
space in a haystack of the Seinpôlle in Grouw, Fryslân a couple of
years earlier where I had made myself scarce to avoid capture by the
Grünen. Patrol boats manned by the Kriegsmarine cruised around
in the area at night, but they never landed a search party of German
police at the Seinpôlle so we had not had a chance to try out our get-
away procedure. Like the Luftwaffe boys, the Kriegsmarine sailors
probably had not been all that keen on this kind of work.

In December, there was a bit more freedom of movement for the
average citizen in The Hague and environs, but our trams stopped
running when the tram personnel went on strike on December 6th,
1944. Until that date, my parents had been using the tram quite
regularly to go shopping in The Hague. When I still had an Ausweis,
I went downtown with my mother once and I'll never forget a little
incident so typical of the mood in those days. The tram was packed
with people for this half-hour trip. When we got in, we had to stand,
but a young German officer jumped up and offered his seat to my
well-dressed mother, with her astrakhan and beret. He got an icy
"Nein, danke," from Mam as she stared the poor man down in her
typical way. The other passengers around us reacted with stony
faces. The officer didn't know what to do and didn't retake his seat.
Nobody else did either and the seat remained empty all the way, as
if it had been contaminated. There were no other stops for quite
a while because the tram was passing through Sperrgebiet (the
prohibited area of the V2 district). After this passage, a woman
selling fish came on board in her Scheveningen black dress with
a white cap, put her basket down, noticed the German officer and
said, "Goeie morgen, lazer straal" ("Good morning, you bastard").
The German smiled and nodded nicely, obviously relieved that
someone talked to him but without the faintest idea what she had
said. Of course, little vignettes like this occurred not only when
the trams were still running but also when the old fish boat still

ventured out from Scheveningen.

During the last few months of 1944, the Resistance in Holland seemed to have matured into a much more coordinated and professional organization, its vital news service in particular. Our trusted Radio Oranje in London had also become a much more reliable and intelligent news source than in previous years, when it exhorted its audience in occupied Holland with all sorts of anti-Nazi propaganda that few people needed. Many listeners in occupied Holland, including my friends and myself, did not tune into Radio Oranje but listened to the BBC or Resistance news sources. When so many of us had to abandon radio news because of the lack of electricity, we turned to the Resistance press. In November, 1944, there were a total of nine prominent newspapers: *Het Parool*, printed and issued separately in Amsterdam, The Hague and Eindhoven; *Trouw*; *Vry Nederland*; *Ons Volk*; *De Geus*; *Voor Koningin en Vaderland*; *De Waarheid*, a Communist paper; *Je Maintiendrai*; and *Oranje Bulletin*. As I mentioned earlier, my brother Nap was the editor of The Hague edition of *Het Parool*. The papers were printed throughout the country right under the nose of the Germans and distributed by couriers and courières of all ages. Few of them were ever caught by the Grünen or the Landwacht. Almost every major community had its own clandestine stencilled newspaper in addition to the regular weekly or monthly papers.

The building of the most prominent daily newspaper in The Hague, the *Haagse Courant*, was blown up by the Germans on September 30th, 1944. Like all major newspapers in occupied Holland, it had been under Nazi control since May, 1940, but its editorial and technical staff didn't toe the line so they lost their building and had to go into hiding. I do not know if the newspaper's presses had been used by the Resistance, but it seems likely.

The Resistance had to get the R.A.F. involved to knock out the national register office of the Netherlands, which stored all the personal data of its population – obviously a well-guarded source of information for the German police and Gestapo, and a prime target of the Resistance. After months of preparations and trials using a maquette of the city, four Mosquitoes set out on April 11, 1944 to destroy the *Kunstzaal Kleikamp* in The Hague, a building near the Peace Palace. It was in this Kunstzaal (arts hall) that the Germans had stored millions of our fingerprints and personal history. From what we heard later, the two first bombs were direct hits. I was told that the next two Mosquitoes did not release their bombs because there was no need for them. A uniquely R.A.F. thrift! I also heard from someone involved in this operation that the Mosquitoes followed a certain street, the Anna Paulowna street, in The Hague as directed by a Dutch navigator who had lived in that quarter. There were sixty-two casualties, mostly German girls.

One of our commissioners at the Institute of Ocean Sciences on the west coast of Canada, Norm Hull, had been a Mosquito pilot during the war and occasionally dropped by in my office on his evening round when I was working late. We had some interesting discussions about the (de Havilland) Mosquitoes. The raid on the Kleikamp building was a standard operation, he told me. The two-man crew spent much more time on preparation and test flights than on the actual sortie, which had to be a surprise in order to be effective. Indeed, work in the Kleikamp building was in full swing in broad daylight when the Mosquitoes struck. Most of Norm Hull's flights were over Norway, where he carried out similar raids. As we talked about his adventures, I wondered how such a quiet and likeable gentleman and his fellow pilots could bring themselves to destroy the lives of dozens of girls who were just doing some desk jobs (*grijze muizen* we called them – grey mice, because of the colour of their uniforms). But then, if these airmen had not carried out their destructive missions, how many Dutch and Norwegian lives might have been lost – valuable women and men like my brother Nap of the "Parool" group, or a teacher at our gymnasium who had had the courage to hide one of his Jewish students?

Except for the purely defensive attacks by the Spitfires on the V2 and V1 launch sites near The Hague and Wassenaar, there was no significant R.A.F. or U.S. Air Force activity north of the Moerdijk and the large rivers separating the allied and German forces. The allies had captured the approaches to the Moerdijk bridges on the seventh of November and the Polish troops under allied command, for some reason, did not attempt to take the bridge intact. They even allowed the German engineers to install the explosives unmolested and to blow up both large bridges. The anticipated military push north across the large rivers by the allies did not happen and likely would not before the next summer. The endless columns of hand carts and wheelbarrows on our highways extended further north as more and more farms simply ran out of food and were saturated with traded goods. It must have been a strange experience for the fighter pilots to look down on, instead of armoured columns, this sad procession of emaciated and desperate people trekking along the highways.

December has always been my favourite month in Holland. First we celebrate Sinterklaas on the fifth of December, when Saint Sinterklaas and his Moroccan helper Zwarte Piet (Black Peter) arrive on a boat in Amsterdam to usher in a national celebration of Sinterklaas' birthday. Schools throughout the country close at noon to give the kids time to welcome the Saint. He visits every family throughout the country on his white horse that night and hands out presents to the good kids, while Zwarte Piet threatens the bad and the good alike with a birch rod and a mean grin. The event is a bit like Santa Claus on this continent, but more spicy. Santa Claus is nice old man; Sinterklaas and his naughty helper are not always nice. Sinterklaas often reprimands Zwarte Piet for his antics and the kids love it because they identify with Zwarte Piet. Dutch immigrants in Canada have tried to import this unique birthday celebration of Sinterklaas without much success. Canadians don't have the same sense of humour. Sinterklaas here in Canada is sometimes called Dutch Christmas, but it has nothing to do with Christmas. Christmas in Holland, at least in my youth, was more religious and is still less boisterous and glitzy than on this continent. In my day, there were no presents. Presents were exchanged during *Sinterklaas avond* (the evening of Sinterklaas) with poems and teasing. Friesland honours its own Saint, Sint Pieter, some day in February.

When our three Canadian-born children were still toddlers, their mother, Alice, and our neighbour, Mimi, sewed a couple of beautiful and elaborate costumes of Sinterklaas and Zwarte Piet, designed after pictures they found in a Dutch magazine. A Dutch friend, Tony, and I dressed as Sinterklaas and Zwarte Piet respectively, performed for the children just as we would have in Holland and had a great time. We even put horse manure in front of the fireplace after the kids set out their shoes to be filled with gifts and went to bed. They didn't believe that Sinterklaas rode a white horse over the rooftops.

During the gloomy 1940-1944 winters, Sinterklaas and Zwarte Piet didn't show up, but some compassionate members of the German administration wanted to do something nice for their oppressed Dutch neighbours and one Sinterklaas, in December, 1941, they ordered an extra ration of... cheese for everyone. Cheese instead of *peper noten* (ginger nuts) strewn by Zwarte Piet, or *speculaas* (spice biscuits) to decorate the mantelpiece? What an insult to our folklore! The Sinterklaas evening in the hunger winter did not lessen the distant thunder in the far south, where the Germans and Canadians were facing each other across our large rivers, nor did the roar of the R.A.F. armadas above us, invisible in the night sky even when the moon was out. After all, how many of the combatants ever heard of that old guy, Sinterklaas?

Christmas Eve didn't stop the hostilities either, but on Christmas day, 1944, all was quiet, finally. I spent Christmas Eve with my parents in our living room, which was kept warm with our improvised wood stove and very heavy velvet drapes. As in every home around our area, our light source was a cotton wick on a small float in a bowl of oil – very simple. One couldn't read by it. I have forgotten what our Christmas dinner consisted of, but I'm sure Mam had scrounged something special. We talked a little bit about Frits, who was somewhere at sea, and the recent events around us, and also about Stien's revelation that her congregation in Wassenaar had been asked by the priest to pray for Hitler. Did the Pope know about this? My mother suggested I read one of her novels to get some idea about the Catholic Church and its politics. It was spooky to sit around that little flame in a small room separated from the rest of our large house by the drapes, which not only kept the cold out, but also any sound. I was watching my father poke in the wood stove to heat a kettle of water; the once ever-so robust man looked scrawny. My mother was playing with her new friend, Duimpje, a Maltese lion dog, which she had acquired a long time after Sobat's death. Our cat, Rode Piraat, had disappeared two weeks earlier. He once stole a steak from the kitchen of our German neighbours and brought it home to everybody's delight, but he might have tried it again and have been caught and killed. We never had any contact with those people so we didn't know. Mam had hunger oedema, caused by malnutrition. If one pushed a finger in her arm, it left a dent in the flesh for some time. Both my parents looked very tired, almost beaten.

As usual during the lack of electricity and the curfew, we turned in at seven p.m. It was minus-three degrees centigrade outside and in my room in the attic, but the cold never bothered me, perhaps due to years of cold showers (thank you, Mr. Amundsen!). I felt like crying, thinking about my parents, but then, what about all those families in The Hague that never received any *Liebesgaben* or smuggled food from local farms? How did those city people manage? Through the open window, I looked down on the houses across the street. There were many tiny little flames in most of the windows. No need for a black-out anymore. I sat down with my two little candles donated by my parents for my hideout and wrote a Christmas story in my diary. It was actually quite upbeat.

Another emotion-filled year was behind us; a year we'd like to forget, but it could have been worse. My parents and brothers had so far survived and we were still in our house. There had been no trace of Rode Piraat since two weeks before Christmas, although I searched the neighbourhood calling him. Sobat and that horrible day when we had to part with her were still on my mind.

The allied troops might have been here by Christmas if it had not been for the miscalculations at Arnhem and in the Belgian Ardennes. The Germans would hang on until their cities had been razed by the thousands of Flying Fortresses and Lancasters that kept crossing our coast day and night on their way to the German industrial centres. The German army was not going to surrender as long as their leaders did not give up and they stalled because they'd have to face execution for their war crimes. In the meantime, what was I going to do? There was no doubt in my mind that I must leave home. Living in the attic had become unbearable; I felt like a caged animal. Practising guitar and mandolin did not go well; it was too cold for the fingers.

More importantly, my departure would provide my parents with an extra food ration voucher. Shortly before Christmas, the Nazi administration had come up with the so-called *nood kaarten* (emergency cards), which had food coupons with new black numbers identifying the place where they had been issued. For instance, Wassenaar's number was 414. They could only be used in the same location where they had been issued. It was a setback for raids on distribution centres by the Resistance to provide railway strikers with food coupons. The coupons were often obtained from "soft" distribution centres with inadequate police protection and were delivered to strikers anywhere in the country. However, the same new regulation made it unnecessary for applicants of a new *nood kaart* to come in person with their identification card. They just had to hand in their old expired card. I don't know which bureaucratic idiot came up with this innovative clause. It targeted the raids on distribution centres, but it was a break for the *onderduikers* (people in hiding) and their hosts. In the case of my parents, they could pick up my new *nood kaart* by just handing over the old expired one even if I wasn't home anymore. So much for the hunger factor. At least I did not have to rob the distribution centres in Wassenaar to steal some cards for my parents. I left that to the professionals.

Then there was the firewood factor and that was not a big deal in Wassenaar. In the cities, it was a crisis; people cut trees in parks and along streets with the most primitive tools, sometimes spending much of a whole day on a little ornamental tree or even tearing out wood blocks in the pavement or asphalt. Firewood was not a problem in Wassenaar with its forests and groves nearby, in particular near our street at the village's edge. The trees in our yard had already disappeared, but I had my eye on the Rommel asparagus north of our van Zuylen van Nijevelt straat, in the large field where, in May, 1940, the German paratroopers had landed. Expecting a similar assault by the allies with gliders, the Germans had planted thousands of ten-foot high oak posts along the coast, with a diameter of about eight inches. During the Normandy operation in June, several allied gliders has crashed on these pointed posts. They were called Rommel asparagus after the German general in charge of coastal defences.

Just after Christmas, there was good ice in the canals north of our street and a dense fog was hanging over the field. The curfew was still in force so, at night, I snuck across our street through someone's yard to the canal north of the street. I tied on my good old Frisian speed skates and skated to the first row of Rommel asparagus, laid down on my tummy and sawed through the very hard oak, keeping the skates on because they had straps and were difficult to tie on if I had to buzz off in a hurry.

I must say that father Jelte kept his tools in top shape. The saw was as sharp as could be, but it still took a while before the post was cut right near the ground, slowly and noiselessly. Then I heard someone nearby doing the same thing with a lot more noise; I crawled and skated over and gave the guy a piece of my mind. He slowed down. I guess it was his first Rommel asparagus too. I dragged my Rommel post home safely and we had some excellent firewood for at least a week in our little room. I did not go back for more because it had thawed the next day (coastal climate), the fog had lifted and the moon was out. Moreover, a German patrol might have noticed the two stumps.

On New Year's Eve, at 23:55, a V2 was launched in Wassenaar to land and explode in London at 00:00 exactly, but almost immediately, it strayed, fell down and exploded in The Hague. There were no casualties because the neighbourhood had just been evacuated. On New Year's Day, we were surprised by a large number of German fighters circling over our village and Valkenburg, apparently to attack an airport in Brabant, the liberated province in The Netherlands.

During the first week of January, 1945, a new campaign by the Germans called for all men between seventeen and forty to report for the Arbeitseinsatz, but there were no *razzias* and I cycled to The Hague on the 3rd of January without noticing any sign of them. I visited Nap with a suggestion to volunteer as a courier for the Resistance through the frontline. Nap told me that I didn't have a hope – too young and inexperienced. "Geen sprake van" was his reaction: "Out of the question." So I got back on my bike to return to Wassenaar before dark. And then it happened. Throughout the year of *razzias* and confiscated bicycles, I had never been caught in a German roadblock, but this time I didn't have my mind on it after my visit to brother Nap and I cycled straight into a trap on the main exit from the city centre, crossing the Prinsesse Gracht. I was somewhat distracted by a large and loud mob of onlookers at the corner of this exit. Suddenly I was confronted by a member of the Feldgendarmerie – a big guy (I think the Feldgendarmerie was the Military Police; they had a white braided sort of necklace) who grabbed the handlebars of my bike. "Ausweis für das Rad!" Of course, I never had an Ausweis für das Rad (permit for my bike) and I tried in vain to show him my expired Ausweis of the Nederland. He didn't buy it and stuck my identification and Nederland Ausweis in his pocket and parked the bike against a lamppost. He stopped another guy who tried to seize the opportunity and cycle past us. Then the German wrote a Schein (a receipt: F 45) and handed it to me together with my ID and the expired Nederland Ausweis. I was devastated and kept staring at my bike leaning against the lamppost only thirty feet away. The mob was screaming at the German. It has always intrigued me how the Germans attracted large, hostile and

vociferous crowds when they did something unpopular and provocative like confiscating bikes and radios, and then failed to disperse the angry mob, in particular in the big cities like Amsterdam
and The Hague.

While the Feldgendarmerie man was writing a Schein for his
second frustrated victim, someone again attempted to cycle past.
The German chased him and all hell broke loose.

"Pak je fiets, meneer, sta daar niet te lullen!" ("Grab your bike.
Don't just stand there!")

Now I had my ID back, so there was a chance. Somehow I felt
like I was floating on this wave of noise. I ran to my bike, jumped
on and took off, never looking back, into an alley and I was gone. I
heard a loud applause behind me. I cycled straight to Nap's house
and handed him the Schein.

"My contribution to your Parool."

"They got your bike?"

"No, it's outside."

It was nice to see my brother really puzzled. We walked into the
living room and I explained. Nap sat down.

"God Allemachtig!"

He asked if the German had tried to shoot me.

"No," I said, "He didn't have time."

I gave credit to the crowd, but that did not seem to surprise
him. He introduced me to his co-workers – an interesting group.
I think that they were working on an edition of *Het Parool*. One
man was not; he was a South African on his way to some mission
in Scandinavia. I had no idea how he managed to travel. His name
was Blinkie. I had to leave, to cycle home before dark. As Nap saw
me to the door, he said, "Je gaat" ("You're on"). He told me that
he had to prepare a few things, including addresses of a couple of
people who lived near the rivers that I had to cross: addresses written on cigarette paper which I had to swallow if caught, Resistance
identification hidden in a piece of bread, and a lengthy document of
the starvation in Holland that had to go to *Het Parool* in Eindhoven
to be forwarded to London. But I would be on my own when crossing the frontline; and I was not to be armed because, as Nap said,

"You don't have a chance. You're dealing with professionals."

I got on my bike and left the big city without getting caught again.

Nap's change of heart in letting his kid brother run documents through the front line was a surprise. I had a talk with Blinkie and wondered if he had something to do with it. I never met him again to find out.

9

JANUARY 1945

I arrived home that same evening; there were no road blocks, no *razzias*, no Spitfires. I patted my bike on its saddle with my humble apologies for almost losing it to the Germans. I stayed there for three days to be with my parents, cleaning my room and storing my stuff, in particular the diaries kept from January 1st, 1940 to January 6th, 1945 with a brief entry on January 7th, followed with an unsolicited remark by a Dutch young lady who managed to pinch my last volume to add a few lines of her own before furtively returning it. Thank you, Miesje Scheurleer! Miesje was one of the Dutch girls in the notorious Japanese concentration camp at Amberawa on the island of Java. She had been spirited out to the Dutch ship *Tarakan*, on which I happened to be serving as an apprentice after the war in Europe.

I told my parents that I was going away. It was difficult. Mam was crying and my father grabbed me by the arm and shook me. He suspected that I was leaving because the three of us together were having difficulty surviving on our rations – particularly my mother with her oedema – and that an extra ration card should see my parents through the hunger winter.

"We should stick together to the end," he said, "whatever the end is."

I had expected my parents' reaction and had no intention of changing my plans. The "food factor" was more a justification to leave than the main reason. I felt totally useless being caged in the attic to avoid the German police, and then, for how long?

I didn't mention Nap's involvement, if any. If something went wrong, my much older brother might take the blame and my father had been skeptical about his involvement with the Resistance, although my father, when he was much younger, surely would have done the same thing. When Nap once asked my parents to hide a Jewish girl, they declined only because they were already hiding me.

I had to somehow indicate to my parents how in the future they would hear from me. I opened my very old box of animal toys which was still around in my room. I selected a rhinoceros and put it on the mantelpiece and told my parents if they heard a friend say something about a rhino, he would have a message from me. Then I went to our neighbours Evert and Vera, who were still getting the daily news from London. I asked them to listen to Radio Oranje's evening news on the forty-one and forty-nine metre bands on Saturday nights and listen for a message from the Rhinoceros. One or two such coded messages from couriers of the Resistance were transmitted to Holland every week and repeated once in the following Saturday's transmission. I had picked the Rhinoceros because I didn't think anybody else would choose such a weird name. Nap had insisted that I pick my own code name because, as he put it, his kid brother never listened to anybody and that I would forget the code name almost immediately unless I had figured it out myself, particularly when I could remember finding it in my old toy box (smart psychology). Evert and Vera told me they'd look forward to hearing about the rhino. What a great couple.

Alea iacta est!

"The die is cast," to quote Caesar when he crossed the Rubicon. There was no turning back. When I recently reviewed my diaries, I scanned the last couple of days for any emotions – fear, or compassion for my worried parents. I found none. There were only a few comments on the absence of traffic signs and Dutch police in The Hague as I had cycled home. Many of the Dutch policemen were not Nazi-friendly and probably had gone into hiding themselves. I also mentioned passing a couple of houses destroyed by the Germans to avenge the death of one of their soldiers found nearby. Perhaps I figured that it was nobody's business to know what went through my mind in those days, but more likely I think I didn't give a damn anymore.

Johan showed up in my garret the last evening I was at home, just when, for the umpteenth time, I was studying a large chart of the system of rivers between South Holland and Brabant, actually forming the frontline between the German and Allied forces (mostly Canadian). I had never been there and was not at all familiar with the tides and currents in the delta. I needed a clear picture of the area in my mind. The chart had to be left at home; all one needed to arouse the suspicion of the Germans at a checkpoint near the delta would be to carry a chart of the rivers straddling the frontline.

Johan looked at the chart and joked, "Ga je daar naar toe?" ("Are you going there?")

I nodded. More questions.

"Wanneer?" ("When?")

"Morgen," I replied. ("Tomorrow.")

He looked a bit more concerned.

"Werkelijk?" ("Are you sure?")

I nodded again, in a way hoping that he'd think I was kidding. I figured he did. If not, he might think that friend Alard was off his rocker, which would have been fine with me too.

I did not mind telling Johan Huibregtse about my intentions; his whole family was rock-solid anti-Nazi. His father, the respected principal of a high school in Wassenaar, even trained the boys in his senior class to disperse to the school's loft at the approach of the German police to catch students (at school!) for the Arbeitseinsatz. He timed the boys' escape to the loft as an exercise. I was less open with my parents than with Johan about my trip because I had yet to figure out how to find my way out of occupied Holland. They already had enough worries about my two brothers....

I left home on my bike Sunday afternoon, January 7th, with my mother in tears, my father puzzled by the lack of any explanation, and myself cycling along the highway to The Hague in a gloomy mood because of the stupid way in which my parents had been left in the dark about my trip. "Why, Ages?" I asked myself. "Could you not have lied that you were cycling to Friesland to stay on the farm in Grouw until the liberation?" Hah! My father would have told it to neighbour Evert who naïvely might have mentioned my suggestion to listen to Radio Oranje in London. In London? Was he not supposed to be going to Grouw? That would really have dumbfounded everybody to the point of thinking that young Ages had lost his marbles. I left it at that and, while trundling along through the outskirts of The Hague, veered off to some side roads to avoid another bike *razzia*. My bike and I arrived safely at Nap's place, this time without a contribution to his revered newspaper.

Nap's house was as busy as ever and I wondered if all this *va-et-vient* of visitors did not arouse the suspicion of the German police or Gestapo in The Hague. The Gestapo had already raided Nap's cover, the "Cheese Export" office, but had not found anything. As an underground newspaper, *Het Parool* had in a couple of years grown from a small handout in Amsterdam to a nationwide organization closely allied with the Resistance. Along with other prominent underground newspapers (*Vrij Nederland* and *Trouw*, for example), it branched out from Amsterdam and The Hague to other centres in the Netherlands as far as Eindhoven. There was little competition from the posh and well-designed news bulletins (such as the *Wervel wind*) dropped by the R.A.F. over occupied Holland because people had more faith in "our own" newspapers. I do not know who financed the creation and distribution of all these competing underground newspapers. Considering the thousands of volunteers among journalists, printers, couriers and teenagers or even children who delivered the papers to our homes at night, they saved millions of dollars or guilders per month in salaries. Of course, there was no income from subscriptions. A nice project for a student in economy or political science: "How the Dutch media survived five years of Nazi occupation."

Nap lived in a normally busy and noisy district of the big city, but the street was empty, even on Sunday. There were no cars and only a few cyclists, wary of another bike *razzia* at street corners.

German military vehicles had disappeared quite a while ago. The Germans were out of fuel themselves, this being the main reason behind the *razzias* for bicycles, including ladies' bikes.

A brotherly pep talk was on Nap's agenda. I had closed my diary at home in Wassenaar (which I have consulted for this episode), but his instructions and warnings are still as vivid in my memory as if it was yesterday. As anticipated, Nap warned me that I had a fifty-fifty chance of surviving the enterprise, but I had to give him credit for not making a dramatic remark that a possible arrest and interrogation might affect his entire Resistance cell in The Hague. Nap had got a kick out of the recovery of my bike a few days ago but warned, "Don't try to pull that off in the war zone where you'll deal with the SS, not with a guy collecting bicycles." He told me to surrender when trapped, not to run. However, he also urged me not to listen to the locals over there who would try to scare me with stories of German machine gun sites, patrol boats and even "waterfietsen" (water bikes peddled noiselessly at night).

"Nonsense," he said. "There are always people who like to spread these rumours to justify why they don't go for it."

He gave me a lot of money in bills to either rent or, more likely, buy a canoe to cross the frontlines at night. He handed me a few addresses in the area of people whom I could trust and who would hide me during the rather frequent local *razzias*. One among them, a police inspector in the little town of Sliedrecht, was connected with the Resistance and I was to contact him right away to go over the tides and currents and the German positions along the rivers. I have forgotten his name but, according to Nap, he was a friend of the family and he'd be all right. The addresses were written on cigarette papers stuffed into my breast pocket. In case of danger, I had to put my head down and swallow them. Nap gave me my *Het Parool* identity card (#92) and the name of my contact in liberated Eindhoven. The card was signed *De Wilde*, Nap's Resistance code name; it was hidden in a small loaf of bread – either baked in or stuffed in. I forget what they told me, but the card did not show. Then there was a document put together by a meeting of doctors in Holland just a day or two earlier detailing the starvation in the big cities like Amsterdam and The Hague. I didn't read all the details, but it looked pretty grim. I hoped that this report by *Het Parool* might help urge the authorities in London to ship or fly food supplies to the starved western provinces and that my trip would not be just a personal adventure. The report was put in the soles of my shoes. There were a couple of other papers, which I didn't read. Together with the document by the doctors, they were to be delivered to *Het Parool* in Eindhoven and forwarded to London. Finally, Nap gave me a false pass that identified me as a member of the Kriegsmarine (the German Navy) on my way to Hellevoetsluis.

Hellevoetsluis was a German navy base for small patrol vessels on the sea arm Haringvliet, close to the entrance to the North Sea. I did not intend to go there, but the pass would help me clear check-points South of The Hague and bridges near Rotterdam on my way to Dordrecht. I'd spend the first night with friends in Dordrecht and head for Sliedrecht the next morning and prepare for the cross-ing. When Nap handed me the fake Kriegsmarine ID, complete with the swastika logo and the signature of some phony German bureaucrat, he emphasized to examine the checkpoint or bridge a bit from a distance before attempting to go through with the false pass. A higher rank officer or a man in civvies (Gestapo) might ask questions.

Nap impressed me. This once so boyish and reckless brother of mine had turned into a really cool guy, totally devoted to the Resistance. He seemed to consider his clashes with the German secret police more as a challenge to outwit his cunning rivals than as a mission to eliminate them. According to Welmoet, he contem-plated going with me to set me up for the crossing, but his associates talked him out of it. I wouldn't have let him anyway. It was a one-man job and would probably involve a kayak, with which he was not familiar.

Another emotional farewell to the family in the early morning of January 8th... I kissed Wil goodbye while she was sitting on the staircase, shivering in her kimono; then I shook hands with a sub-dued Nap while he handed me my bike. (No, reader, in those days, three generations ago, Dutch men didn't hug other men, not even after scoring a goal in soccer.)

And off we went, my old Bailey with its real rubber tires and I, into the unknown. The streets in The Hague were empty and I was not worried about bike *razzias* because it was simply too early to expect people on bikes at this hour, other than those who went to work and had a legitimate permit for their bike. Bike *razzias* were most profitable for the Germans when people ventured out to visit or to go shopping, but certainly not on early Monday mornings. Indeed, I cleared the city smoothly and entered the highway South to Rotterdam in no time, exchanging thumbs up greetings with other early bikers riding in the opposite direction. It was a beautiful, crisp winter morning. There was no need to follow a bicycle path along the highway; one had the highway all for oneself. There were no cars in sight or even motorbikes. I mused, without irony, what a blessing it would be to humankind if the world ran out of oil. I took both hands off the handlebars and zigzagged along the well-paved highway, singing at the top of my voice.

After cycling past the outskirts of Delft and Rotterdam, I soon sighted the cityscape of Dordrecht across the river Merwede. Near the approaches of the highway bridge to the city, I got off the bike to sit in the grass and eat some of the cheese that Nap had given me for the trip and to watch the bridge. A couple of pedestrians and cyclists went across and were stopped by a German soldier to check their IDs. He did not frisk anybody or seem to ask questions so I cycled to the bridge, handed the Kriegsmarine ID to the German, who glanced at it and wished me "eine gute Reise." While crossing the bridge, I noticed a very large aircraft bomb attached to a girder outside the bridge deck – obviously rigged to blow up the bridge in case of a future allied push from the South to Rotterdam.

I arrived at my friend's residence unannounced (telephone connections did not exist in the winter of 1944/45). Daad and Ees Haks used to have a horse carriage business in Soestdijk, my birthplace, and served weddings and funerals or moved households. Like my grandfather in De Lemmer's devotion to commercial sailing ships at the turn of the century, Daad Haks never abandoned his horses to change to automobiles and lost his business to a more aggressive and less romantic competitor who switched to cars. The Haks and Ages families remained close friends after my parents left Soestdijk. Daad and Ees eventually moved to Dordrecht, where they became associated with some other business, but we never lost contact.

Compared to the turbulent way of life in Wassenaar and The Hague, Dordrecht's calm was almost unreal. There were no V2s thundering up on their way to London or down to Wassenaar when they misfired; no Spitfires circled around over our heads here in Dordrecht, looking for any attractive target in our streets like hawks hunting field mice. Here I did not see any signs "Vorsicht, Minen Gefahr" marking minefields, or Rommel asparagus, or machine gun emplacements. So which city really was part of the frontline, Den Haag and suburb Wassenaar or Dordrecht?

The two communities had one common problem: no electricity. So again I turned in with candlelight. Just before my departure from Wassenaar, I read a brief note in my diary that all men between certain ages living on the Dordt Island (including Dordrecht) had to leave, likely because of the threat of an allied invasion. Men living on the Island? I had started to have moments of doubt about the wisdom of taking documents across the rivers for the Resistance instead of leaving the job to any of these locals who'd be more familiar with the area and the currents. Perhaps Daad could help me find someone… No, no, no way, Ages. There is no turning back. "Je gaat" (vid. page 113). Tomorrow morning.

We spent much of the evening reminiscing about Soestdijk, where the Haks family lived for generations and where I was born after my parents and two brothers returned from a year in Switzerland. The relaxed country style of Soestdijk was most likely the reason why crown Princess Juliana and her popular husband Prince Bernhard chose Soestdijk as their residence and had their two first daughters, Beatrix (at present, Queen of the Netherlands) and Irene, attend the village school instead of a private learning institute. People in Soestdijk loved the unassuming Royal Family. We also talked a little bit about that memorable summer in 1931 when my parents took seven-year-old junior Alard (myself) to Soestdijk and I ended up in hospital. I was sitting on the bike carrier behind Daad and tried to stop the running bike by sticking my left leg in the spokes. I broke my left leg, but not without bending the rear fork. Off to the hospital in Leiden went the little innovator. What I remember most of all about this loused-up summer was that the surgeon did not put me comfortably to sleep during the operation but pulled my hair and screamed at me while putting the fibula and/or the tibia together again. It was apparently the way a surgeon toughened up his patients in those days. Many years later, during the occupation, Daad's mother (then a widow we called Haksie) once hid me in her little house when I cycled through her village on my way to Friesland and almost ran into a *razzia* for the Arbeitseinsatz.

Sliedrecht

I had told Daad and Ees about my intention to cross the rivers and they insisted that I stay at their place until I had become familiar with the area. However, in those days, one could not enjoy anyone's hospitality more than a couple of days because of the shortage of food in our households. The "food factor" became more critical in our social life than the mode of transportation – even a bike.

First of all, I had to go to Sliedrecht to get advice from the police inspector on the river currents and the German positions and patrols. I also needed to get a *kano*. A kano like the one I had in Friesland is an old-fashioned wooden version of a kayak, slower and less elegant. A dictionary translates the word into canoe, but a canoe in Canada is a wider and more stable version moved with separate side-paddles while a kanoist and kayaker use one long paddle with a blade at each end. Kanos are often home-built out of marine plywood with a solid centre layer. I built three of these ten-foot boats for my kids in exchange for them getting their swimming diplomas.

To commute to Sliedrecht in the next couple of days, I had to pass through the same check point twice a day in either direction with the risk that a German guard, after wishing me "eine gute Reise" to Hellevoetsluis, and on to the North Sea, would check me again on my way to Sliedrecht nearby the very next day. This snag was exactly what Nap had cautioned me about when he handed me the Kriegsmarine pass. However, I was lucky. The guards took turns throughout the day and were too bored to be nosey. And that big bomb was still hanging onto its girder. What a monster!

My recollection of Sliedrecht and the people I contacted is rather vague after sixty years. No diary exists to be consulted; I later swallowed the names and addresses of my contacts with the cigarette papers on which they were scribbled. Whatever other helpful information might have been in my bag was lost when the boat capsized, although the documents were saved, because I had them under my pullover.

The meeting with the police inspector turned out to be the most vital part of the entire undertaking. On his chart, he showed me the crossing the way he would go about it, through every step from Sliedrecht to the south shore of the very wide waterway, Hollands Diep, near the Moerdijk bridges. He dismissed my plan to start moving upstream from Sliedrecht along the Beneden Merwede and then around the northeast corner of the Dordt Island, to catch the combined southwest ebb and river flow, and end in Lage Zwaluwe on the south shore of the Hollands Diep. There were German positions near this north east corner of Dordt Island. Instead, he suggested (insisted) I somehow cross the Beneden Merwede unnoticed to a farm on the south shore and, with the help of a farmer and a couple of his workers, carry the kano over land, clearing the German positions at night, and then launch the boat in the Nieuwe Merwede. He showed me the location of the farm on the south shore of the Beneden Merwede and assured me that they'd help carry the boat. However, it was this "crossing unnoticed" term that worried me. Not without reason, as I would find out.

The crossing should not be attempted later than two nights after our meeting because of the new moon and the forecast of a clear sky to let the constellations give me some guidance. I agreed with him on that last point after my experience with the kano at night on the Frisian lakes. The inspector mentioned that he knew a young man who lived in Sliedrecht with his mother and had a two-person kano. He might be interested in joining me for the crossing. I'd find out the next day.

I met my prospective partner and he seemed keen on going, although his mother tried to talk him out of this venture. Nevertheless, we agreed on the next late afternoon, the 12th of January, after we'd prepared the kano in the morning. Unfortunately, when I returned from my last night with Daad and Ees in Dordrecht that morning, I learned that he had changed his mind. His mother had won and I couldn't really blame her. I was running out of time and so were the new moon and the possibility of a clear night sky with Orion to show me the way. And I still had to find a boat.

Disheartened and actually quite angry, I cycled around for a while until I spotted some commotion on the road along the dike. Another *razzia* for the Arbeitseinsatz! A couple of guys raced past me, away from the commotion. I noticed some green uniforms in the crowd, didn't bother to find out what it was all about and had just enough time to reach the house of the people listed on my little cigarette papers, which I had not yet swallowed and had checked the day before. A woman opened the door. I told her that my Parool ID was still in a piece of bread and she told me not to bother digging it out but to go to the attic. All I can remember of that "visit" was that I stayed in the attic during the night, probably had something to eat, and that we had a long discussion by candlelight. The house was not searched. I also remember her telling me to go right back home and stay out of trouble. This woman, in her thirties, was a character and probably quite an asset to the Resistance. She didn't discuss her own activities.

When I eventually returned to Holland several months later, my mother mentioned that she had a dream about me lying in bed and talking to a woman with long hair sitting beside the bed. She mentioned this flash to my father who, after earlier similar events, had started to write down her dreams. The dates were the same. I don't know about the times. When brother Frits returned after the war, not months but years after leaving home, my mother had a similar question for him. She once had a dream that he was hit by a tank. Frits recalled that indeed he had been hit by a British tank being unloaded from his ship in Alexandria, Egypt, for the British Army (the Desert Rats), which was engaged in a battle with the Germans. The tank fell out of the cargo slings and fortunately just grazed him while he was standing near the edge of the cargo hold. My father wrote down her visions somewhat skeptically, but he became a believer when my mother saw in her dream a close friend (an author as well) walking into a flooded ditch in the middle of the night. My father got on his bicycle and found her in the ditch near the institute where she was being treated. These observations were no mere fantasies. Some readers may dismiss them as sensational poppycock and may start to question the veracity of the other somewhat unusual episodes I've described. However, my mother did not lie and her analytical husband and three sons would not readily have accepted any such sixth sense or supernatural communications unless their existence was supported by actual observations – the data. And the data were there.

A Wild Night to Freedom

Still undecided on what to do next, I cycled along the north shore of the Beneden Merwede to get some idea of the currents as well as of any activity by the Germans near the northeast point of Dordt Island. The current seemed to be quite manageable for a boat trying to cross the river from Sliedrecht to the farm pointed out by the police inspector. The tides most likely had little effect upon the riverflow about forty kilometres upstream from the mouth. There were no Germans in sight near the NE point of Dordt Island but, all in all, the inspector's advice to avoid the NE point seemed well taken because of its strategic location for the Germans. They'd keep an eye on any boat traffic around that point, especially at night.

I decided to go for it and get a boat even if it had to be stolen. After cycling back to Sliedrecht, I walked down the ramp to a boat house on the shore close to the town, looked through the windows and spotted a fairly large kano, possibly for two people. It looked like a pretty crummy contraption, but it would last for much of the night. I had to break in just before dark, drag it out to the water and cross the river to the farm in semi-darkness. A paddle was lying nearby. I cycled back to the Parool lady, told her to keep my bicycle as a token of my gratitude and quickly took off before she tried to talk me out of it again. It was sad to part with my bike, but I left it in good hands and, who knows, some day I might retrieve it.

It was getting darker when I returned to the boathouse near the town. I walked down the ramp but couldn't force the door open so I smashed one of the little windows above the door lock, reached inside and unlocked the door. Just as I started dragging the boat out, there were footsteps on the ramp outside. Hiding behind a pile of wooden panels, I watched an old man enter, probably the watchman investigating the noise of broken glass. The man must have noticed the smashed little window on the door and the glass on the floor, but he did not look any further and left. Assuming that he would not return, I dragged the kano out into the small harbour, put the bag (or the little cane suitcase – I forget which was on my bicycle carrier) with some spare clothes in the boat. I got in the kano, grabbed the paddle and . . . it broke into two. I couldn't believe it. But all was not lost yet. I had the choice of either climbing out of the boat and trying to swipe another paddle in the boathouse, or keeping one half in the boat as a spare and paddling with the other half, switching sides from port to starboard as one would paddle a canoe. The second way is slower but along the Nieuwe Merwede it would not make much difference because the current and winds should be in my back much of the night. My main concern was to stay in midstream because both shores were controlled by the Germans. I do not remember whether I found another paddle before leaving the harbour or kept the two halves of the first paddle.

Jutting out some hundred feet into the river was a high break-water to protect the little harbour. I set course to the distant south shore and, sheltered by the pier, kept an eye on any leaks in the boat because it must have been out of the water several months.

"HALT, WOHIN GEHST?" ("Stop. Where are you going?")

I looked up. A German on the pier. This on top of it all.

"Kartofflen holen!" I shouted back. ("Getting potatoes.") I pointed to the south shore. "Dort." ("There.")

"Ja, mal sicher," he said sarcastically. ("Yeah, sure.")

"Gewisz, gewisz," I called and waved the paddle at him. ("Certainly, certainly.")

"This is it," I thought, forgetting to eat the cigarette papers with the addresses in my breast pocket.

However, while paddling along and trying to keep away from the big rocks at the bottom of the pier, I glanced up and noticed that he had not yet taken his gun off his shoulder, nor did I hear the click of the rifle bolt. While clearing the tip of the pier, I looked back and saw him walking away. The guy could have finished me off but, being by himself, he followed his conscience rather than Nazi doctrine. If this encounter had been in The Hague, I think it might have been lethal.

It took about half an hour to paddle to the farm on the south shore and it was not difficult to locate, even in the dark. I pulled the boat up, knocked on the door and found the family and some farmhands gathered around the dinner table. After introducing myself, I told the farmer about the discussion with the police inspector in Sliedrecht; he supported the inspector's views. He and his men also agreed to help carry the boat across the NE tip of Dordt Island, a distance of about five kilometres. I was invited for dinner and after the last couple of weeks in hunger country, I wolfed down the best traditional meal ever, to the joy of the family. In case of the threat of another war, I'd start farming!

Two young men (I believe a son of the farmer and a farmhand) carried the kano with me to the shore of the Nieuwe Merwede. Even though they knew the trail well, the pace was slow in the darkness. We didn't talk because of the possible presence of a German patrol in this noman's land. At temperatures between -3 to -5 degrees centigrade, the ground was hard under a beautiful moonless sky with little wind. We reached the shore of the Nieuwe Merwede after a couple of hours and put the boat down on the beach. I whispered a profound "bedankt" and they wished me the best of luck. I handed them all of Nap's money in a big wad, a considerable amount, but they refused to accept anything. I pointed out that whatever happened, I didn't need that money any more and that they might want to donate it to the Resistance or something. They accepted.

So here is to you two guys who took a considerable risk to help a total stranger. Without your help, I'd never have made it this far.

After the two men disappeared into the darkness, I sat down a little while to have a rest and to reflect a bit. The other side of the river was invisible, but the kano with its bright yellow deck midstream in the river might contrast with the dark river surface and needed to be camouflaged. I put some branches over the deck, intertwining them to make it look like a floating tree. Then I sat down in my floating tree and pushed off. Even the small surface waves set up by the following light wind swept the camouflage right off and I had no choice but to continue on and stay in the centre of the river, which was a bit dicey because it was difficult to see the low shores on either side. I once heard some German voices on my port bow (to the east), but they did not spot the kano, or didn't look. There were no search lights anywhere along the shore, or even any high-powered flashlights. Before leaving the beach, I had roughly lined up Orion ahead of me with Polaris behind me to true north and I had no problem staying midstream with them as a guide. Then, unexpectedly, there was no shore on either side anymore. The boat was in open water and seemed to be being pushed westward by the current. I could not imagine having entered the much wider Hollands Diep that quickly. While I was still trying to figure out where I was heading, a couple of very large rocks loomed up ahead, the boat capsized and dumped me. I was chest high in water and climbed onto the rocks, looking for the boat. It was gone, dragged out by the current. The rocks were part of a breakwater pointing north on an east-west shore. I stumbled along on the icy rocks, reached the shore and looked around. Standing out in the distance against the lower westerly night sky was the silhouette of a large bridge with a couple of its broken spans in the water. The Moerdijk Bridges! Now I knew where I was, how I got there and where I had to go. It would be a long and difficult walk.

The speed at which the boat had been carried down the Nieuwe Merwede and across the two and a half kilometre-wide Hollands Diep was a surprise. The Nieuwe Merwede joins another, smaller river, the Amer, to discharge into the Haringvliet near the village Lage Zwaluwe, five kilometres east of the Moerdijk bridges. Lage Zwaluwe was the village where I originally wanted to land, but I would never have made it because of the strong westerly outflow into the Haringvliet near this village. Luckily, the inspector in Sliedrecht and the farmer had had other ideas. Both suggested the overland shortcut.

All this analysing didn't sit too well with my freezing legs so I started to walk west to the Moerdijk bridges, following a narrow trail along the dike. It must have been around midnight (I had no watch) when I reached the foot of the Moerdijk bridges, but I still did not know if the Germans had left or were holding on to a bridgehead on the south shore. I turned left on a road parallel to the rails leading to the bridges and walked through a mass of burnt-out tanks, vehicles and equipment, ghastly evidence of the Germans' last stand before retreating north across the bridge or with boats. Following the road and the rails south, away from the bridges, I touched a wire stretched low across the road and set off an explosion about ten feet away. A booby trap or perhaps a warning flare? I did not feel the sting of any shrapnel and a day later didn't notice anything else on my hands or head except a few scratches, probably caused by clambering around on the breakwater.

After the blast, I walked more slowly, with both hands just above the ground for a while. I stepped over a couple more wires close by, one of them right across the rails. Further away from the bridge, there seemed to be no more of the traps. I was mentally too drained to keep worrying anymore about such threats anyway, or about the sudden RATATATAT! of a Sten gun nearby. I heard some voices and promptly dove into a ditch with ice at the bottom.

"Aufstehen, heraus!"

So the Germans were still around...

This time, I didn't forget about my cigarette papers with the addresses of the Resistance people in Sliedrecht but swallowed them quickly while lying flat on my belly. The soldiers found me with a flashlight.

"Aufstehen!" they said once more.

I looked up and could vaguely see them outlined against the night sky. Except their helmets were not German; they were the English model. Then I heard them speak English to each other. CANADIANS. My God, I'd made it!

I got up and stood there with my head down so they could not see my tears. One of them was Dutch, of the Prinses Irene Brigade – probably their interpreter. This Brigade consisted of a significant contingent of Dutch people who had escaped to England during the war and served in the forces. I asked him why they had yelled at me in German, but he explained that they were looking for a German pilot who had bailed out of his fighter aircraft when it was shot down. They had come to investigate the explosion and the flash, but they had not set any flares and figured it had been a booby trap. He made the startling observation that there still might be some hidden landmines lurking near the bridges' approaches, but that the ground had hardened enough after several days of freezing weather to support my light weight without setting them off. I had assumed that landmines could be set for vehicles differently than for personnel.

We walked a few kilometres to the little village of Zevenbergse Hoek where the Canadians were quartered in the presbytery, a large house with several tanks and trucks parked all over the yard. The corporal gave me some dry clothes as well as an army coat and put me on a chesterfield in front of the fireplace. They made me a cup of real tea – actually a canned mixture of tea leaves, sugar and dried milk to be put into hot water. They offered me a cigarette, a Wild Woodbine, which came in green boxes of ten. Having won a bet with my father that I would not smoke before turning nineteen, I now had my first puff. Not all that great. My hosts told me that the Wild Woodbines were a cheap brand, only smoked by the military, and to wait for American brands.

A member of the tank crew walked in, wiped the oil off his hands

with an old rag and sat in front of the fireplace to have a cup of
coffee. He had a badge on his shoulder with the words "Manitoba
Dragoons." I recognized him right away as Native Indian: dark
complexion, black hair and a somewhat flattened nose. He could
have been the descendent of my childhood hero, Winnetou, the
tribal Chief about whom the famous Karl May had written several
children's books known to every boy in the Netherlands and most
likely in other European countries too. Which old-timer does not
remember the exploits of Winnetou, with his Silberbüchse (silver
carabine) and his cowboy friend, Old Shatterhand? I even had
Winnetou's bust on my wall. Of course, in those days, we had yet to
be introduced to the term "First Nation."

The Manitoba Dragoon asked me many questions about Holland
and I had problems answering with my broken English; it did not
seem to bother him. I asked why there were so many bullet holes in
the ceiling and he promptly compared the quality of Canadian Sten
guns (repeating rifles) with their German counterparts.

"If you put a fokkink Canadian gun on the floor with its fokkink
butt down, then the fokkink gun would release its fokkink bullets
all at once, but a jerry gun would not," he explained.

I was under the impression that Fokkink was the Canadian brand name of the Sten gun until I later started to realize that, with a slightly different spelling, this adjective applied to almost everything in the otherwise so rich English language. Other young Dutchmen with whom I travelled to England on a Royal Navy vessel a few weeks later were equally puzzled and had to be enlightened by an amused Dutch official in charge of our transfer to England to enlist in the Dutch navy or merchant navy.

This, my first acquaintance with the Canadians, was quite an experience. They were worlds apart from the rigid discipline of the Germans, or even of the Dutch. They didn't salute; an officer, barely distinguishable from a private, was called by his first name. As far as I could make out, they were volunteers and seemed to come from the same region or province. Their uniforms were something else: a battle dress and a beret – a great idea and quickly adopted by the Dutch military at the end of the war. Their spoken English differed from the BBC enunciation with which I had become familiar during the earlier years of the occupation. They had had a taste of liberating our country when they moved through Brabant and they were looking forward to meeting the Dutch girls north of the rivers. They surely would not be disappointed.

Shortly after daybreak, two officers arrived in a Mercedes, badly shot up with a broken windshield and the German marking painted over. They were with the intelligence, one English, one Dutch. They interviewed me for a couple of hours. Being half asleep, I don't remember the details, but they had the papers which I had handed to the patrol. They were particularly interested in the V2 operation and I had no problem filling them in. The Dutchman in the patrol had already warned me to expect interviews because most of the line-crossers came from nearby, not from Wassenaar with its V2s.

During the day, I wandered around a bit, talking with our Canadian liberators or hanging around the fireplace and listening to their many stories about their Normandy landing and their campaign through France and Belgium. They were pretty casual about it all – no heroics. At times, they were a bit too casual, such as when it came to blasting away at centuries-old buildings or toppling a church tower with a couple of dynamite charges. Of course, compared to Europeans, Canadians do not have very many historic buildings and may not understand Europeans' sensitivity about their destruction.

Another car arrived later in the day to take me to Tilburg. If I remember rightly, it was on this trip that I witnessed a spectacular feat of modern aircraft aerobatics. A V1 was put-putting by, probably on its way from the occupied Eastern Netherlands to the newly reopened harbour in Antwerp. An R.A.F. fighter followed the V1 until it flew side by side with the unmanned flying bomb, then tipped the little wing of the V1 with its own wing. The V1 flipped, dove to the ground and exploded. According to my British companions, some fighters had been rigged with reinforced wings and the pilots assigned to this job had specialized for the manoeuvre.

I was taken to camp 030 near Tilburg, a large hall to accommodate line-crossers – people who had lost their homes on one side of the hall and arrested Dutch Nazis waiting for trial on the other side of a barbed wire fence. I was assigned a bunk bed with a little cupboard to store my belongings of which, of course, I had none. The hall was packed with people reading or playing cards. My neighbours told me that, after a few weeks, they were still waiting for an interview. I started to worry. After all this trouble to become a free man, there I was, sitting on a bunk bed, "waiting to be processed." However, a nearby door opened and two uniformed men came in; one looked at a notebook and called, "Ages, Alard?" I jumped up calling, "here!" and joined the men. They were from the British R.A.F. They drove me to a large airport – I think it was called Gilze Rijen. It had been a Dutch military base before the war.

I'll never forget the awesome display of air power at that airport. "How could the Germans ever have dreamed of winning the war?" was my first thought as we drove past row after row after row of Spitfires, Hurricanes, Typhoons, Mosquitoes, to name just a few, being serviced or taxiing onto the runway to take off.

We stopped at a hangar and I was taken to an anteroom to meet a couple of officers of the Intelligence or Security, I think. They returned my Resistance ID and other IDs but kept the false Kriegsmarine pass. We had a long talk about the crossing. Then they took me into the hangar where they showed me a topographical map of Wassenaar as large as several ping-pong tables. They told me to take as long as I wanted and to call them when I was familiar with the area. It took me quite a while; I was absolutely dumbfounded by all the details that had probably been collected by the planes I had mentioned in my diaries watching them circle at a great altitude without strafing or bombing. The intelligence guys asked me to locate our house, the school and other points of interest. Then they called in a few pilots. I think they knew Wassenaar as well as I did. We spent much of the day and the following morning discussing a variety of aspects related to the V2. It was interesting. They asked for some details about the launching pads, which I did not know, but other queries were no problem to answer: the trucks passing by the house at night, the misfires, the base, V2s going in the wrong direction, the route taken by the V2 truck, the personnel and fuel truck and the times of passage, weather conditions when there was a misfire, etc. It was news to them that, some days, four out of eight rockets misfired, but what surprised the pilots most was my remark that the Spitfires did not always hit the target.

"How could you tell?"

"Because right after the Spitfires had shot up the pad and left, another V2 took off from the same spot."

The observation was not appreciated.

The next afternoon, after more interviews, I was picked up by Nap's counterpart in Eindhoven, Nico v.d. Sande Bakhuyzen, who took me to the Hesselink family with whom I stayed until my departure to England a couple of weeks later. Dr. Hesselink was one of the directors of Philips; apart from his charming wife, there were two dynamic daughters in the family, Camie and Marijke, and their much younger brother, Henk. Earlier, I had notified the Parool people in Eindhoven that I had arrived and would appreciate that a message be transmitted by the BBC's Radio Oranje in London to notify my parents and my brother Nap's Parool, under my resistance code "Rhinoceros," on the following first and second Saturday evenings on the forty-one and forty-nine m band. As I found out later, they did send the message and, as he had promised, our neighbour Evert was listening in his little hideout and received it.

Map of escape route

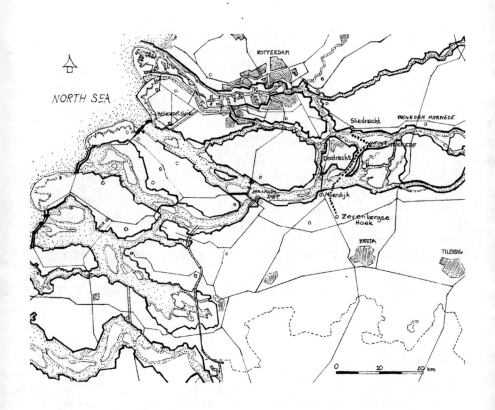

10

FOUR CITIES WORLDS APART

Eindhoven

At the elementary school in Wassenaar, we took geography from the principal, Mr. Heeroma, and were told the province south of Holland, Noord Brabant, was too infertile for agriculture or cattle and turned to industry, manufacturing light bulbs (Philips) and trucks (DAF) early in the 20th century. With a present population of two hundred thousand, Eindhoven has become one of the largest industrial centres of Western Europe. Unlike almost all cities in the Netherlands, it is not known for any heritage buildings. If there were such tourist attractions, they would have been destroyed by allied bombers during the operation Market Garden, Montgomery's attempt to capture Arnhem before the winter. When Monty's daring push had to be abandoned, some young Dutch men living north of the Rhine were stranded in liberated Eindhoven, but, like myself, were welcomed by the Hesselink family later in the winter.

Apart from hosting some of us stranded men and line crossers, the Hesselinks also provided a pied-à-terre for an occasional lonely officer from far away South Africa and Australia, entertained admirably by daughters Camie and Marijke. As a guest of the family, it intrigued me how many people from several members of the Commonwealth had volunteered to do battle with the Nazis.

I didn't see much of Dr. Hesselink, probably because he had his hands full rebuilding the Philips organization after the liberation of Eindhoven. He was quite a guy. One evening after dinner, I was invited to his home office. I took a seat in front of his impressive, very large and well-organized desk and waited politely until he put his papers down to address me.

"Alard," he said, "I noticed that you greeted our dinner guest, Captain Jones, with 'goodbye' when he arrived. You don't say goodbye to a guest when he arrives; you say hello." Then he turned to his papers again.

I apologized and consulted Marijke on this matter and indeed, I had to improve my English. Several years later, I met Marijke again in New York during a short visit of the *Tabian*, a vessel I was on as third mate. She was working for the Dutch Consul and I believe she had written the Nederland Line to learn when I would be in town. We had dinner in an Italian restaurant. I was sorry to hear that her mother had passed away – a great lady, with a great family.

A few days after arriving in Eindhoven, I became a member of a committee interviewing line-crossers. My job was to verify remarks on their activities in the Resistance because there had been cases of fake fugitives, i.e., Nazis on the run. A new agency for recruiting war volunteers was also established in Eindhoven. I applied for pilot training and went through several tests before being accepted, but I promptly shifted to the navy or merchant navy because of my training at the KvdZ. It was a bit of a disappointment not to join the Spitfire elite, but it would also be nice to be on a ship, preferably in the merchant navy without the navy's boring discipline! So, after a few more days in Eindhoven, I kissed Mrs. Hesselink goodbye and was put on an army truck to Antwerp, which had just opened its harbour when the fairway through the Western Schelde had been cleared by the Canadians after some of the fiercest fighting of the war. The truck picked up a few more passengers, navigation and engineering graduates from nautical schools as well. They were living in Brabant when the allies liberated that province. I felt like a vagabond compared to those kids, who were much better equipped to go to sea. However, that was all straightened out by the head office of the Ned Shipping, the administration looking after the wartime Dutch Merchant fleet in London and New York.

In Den Anvers (Flemish for the Dutch Antwerpen – Antwerp in English), we spent the night in a large empty warehouse with the

usual war-type cardboard windows. We shared part of a top floor
with a group of American truck drivers, all black, who drove trucks
between the coast of France and Antwerp or some other city. These
guys were tireless jokers, never stopped giggling and kept us awake
and wondering how they managed to drive a convoy of army trucks
all the way from the coast to Antwerp and still keep telling jokes
afterwards.

The odd explosion of a V1 or V2 in the city didn't help either and
we were happy to leave the noisy night behind us and have a super
breakfast with money generously handed to us by a Dutch official
in Eindhoven. One of the boys, in spite of our warnings, ate too
much and dropped on the street bleeding from the mouth and was
taken to a hospital by an ambulance. He didn't come back. We
embarked on an LCT (landing craft tanks), which took us along
the Western Schelde into the North Sea en route to London. There
were barrage balloons attached to barges all along the Thames
against Luftwaffe intruders. They were serviced by WREN women
(Women's Royal Navy Service) – a fascinating sight. We disembarked near London and were taken to a hotel by the Dutch official
who had accompanied us during the entire voyage. I shared a very
comfortable room with Bob Potjer, son of captain Potjer of the
Nederland Line's flagship, the *Oranje*, then a hospital ship carrying
wounded Australian and New Zealand troops from the Middle East
to their home country. The next morning, I went to the office of the
Ned Shipping to inquire about my brother Frits. They didn't know
him, but apparently they informed the office in New York about
my arrival in London. The kind people in the Ned Shipping office
provided me with a fair amount of money and even with a black
battledress. They also gave me a hat with the emblem of a daisy
(daisy in Dutch is *margriet*, also the name of the Dutch princess,
the patroness of the merchant navy).

*The author, during and after
the Hunger Winter*

London and the Queen Mary

London had been a city under siege ever since the Luftwaffe's first raid on the London docks on June 28, 1940. While my room-mate Bob Potjer and I went for a stroll in the city's centre during our stay in the Ambassador's Hotel, I kept thinking about a dramatic newspaper photo clipping in my diary showing fire fighters battling the fires with dozens of hoses lined up side by side. It must have been a living hell, especially at night during the severe 1940/1941 winter. We were no strangers to the sight of burnt out and collapsed buildings, but we were surprised by the resilience and the almost casual attitude of the people in this stricken city. While Bob met his father, captain Potjer, who was on leave from the Oranje, I ran into a couple of my other travel companions and joined them for lunch in Lyon, a self-service place and one of the several restaurants open for business. Just after taking our plates to our table, we were startled by an ear-shattering explosion nearby, bringing several higher cardboard windows to the floor. A V2! Just five minutes after it must have left the site in Wassenaar. We immediately took cover under the table, but, to our surprise and embarrassment, nobody else did likewise and we could not help noticing that people at tables next to ours didn't even look up or stop their conversations. We were told later that a building nearby had crumbled and that there had been casualties. The captain treated Bob and me to a more quiet lunch the next day. The Spitfires over Wassenaar must have been a bit more on the ball.

After the routine medical exam required to enlist in the navy or merchant navy, I was again interviewed by the intelligence in London, about the V2s of course, but also with more detailed questions about the route I had taken for a virtually unhindered crossing. At the Ned Shipping office, I received more excellent clothing, some of it knitted by Dutch communities in South America, accompanied by appropriate messages and poetry. I lunched with two Dutch gentlemen whose names and functions in the (exiled) Dutch government I do not recall. They suggested a visit with the Queen Wilhelmina. The Queen sometimes received people who had escaped occupied Holland across the North Sea or overland through France and Spain to England and who could keep her up to date with conditions and events in her country. Line-crossers from the area near her residence in The Hague had become a rarity and someone's arrival from Wassenaar prompted these two officials to arrange a visit with the Queen. I told them that of course I'd be honoured. Having listened in awe to my father's stories about his conversations with Willemien during his beach walks, I figured that it would be nice to tell him that he wasn't the only one in the family to occasionally communicate with Her Majesty!

Unfortunately, the Ned Shipping people in London had other ideas. They had arranged a meeting with another Queen. They had booked me on the *Queen Mary* to leave Greenock the next morning for New York and I was scheduled to leave London with the night train that same afternoon. Well. One Queen too many, Ages. Cool it!

Apart from missing an audience with Her Majesty, leaving London so soon saddened me a bit. This city had character. Day and night, it had withstood the furious attacks by the ugly Heinkels 111 (admittedly not any uglier than the square-nosed R.A.F. Lancasters), but its citizens still had some energy left to host the thousands of foreign soldiers, pilots and seamen taking a break from their mission to bring the Nazis to their knees. It was quite an emotional experience for a young Dutchman like me to wander around in the ruined streets of the old city and read the shoulder badges of all those military passers-by from many parts of the world – Australia, U.S.A., Norway, Poland, Canada, even Brazil. Why did they do it? These people were too well informed in their democratic countries to fall for a slogan or a screaming dictator. Several Canadians I talked to after crossing into Brabant told me they hadn't given much thought to what motivated them. They "just went" because a neighbour or friend had signed up, or for adventure. But still, they were volunteers and they didn't go back until the job had been done. The Canadians were called the "mud-borne" troops to distinguish these sluggers from the motorized American troops advancing much faster in the interior.

I boarded the train to Greenock together with three more graduates: one an apprentice from a nautical school like me and two from
engineering schools. It was an all-night journey covering about six
hundred kilometres. The train was packed, many people sitting all
night on their luggage or on the floor. A few blue lights helped
the passengers to move around a bit in the darkness. Of course,
there were no lights in the villages we passed, but the darkness was
a slight inconvenience compared with travelling in Holland, where
trains had not run at all since September.

We arrived in Greenock in the early morning and, as expected,
it was raining in this dreary part of the country. But there she
was, the gigantic *Queen Mary*, one of the largest ocean liners of the
Cunard White Star, the company that once had generously sent me
a fittingly enormous poster after brother Nap had "helped" his kid
brother write a letter in really good English to the Cunard. What
a surprise the response was. The real *Queen Mary* was a different
surprise: she did not have the black and red funnels. They were
war-time grey – like all merchant men.

Grey or camouflage, it was a thrill to get in one of the launches
and head for our cross-Atlantic liner. The launch tied up to a gangway lowered from the ship and we climbed up to one of the passenger decks and found the cabin marked on our tickets. We had
been given one cabin with four bunk beds. The *Queen Mary* had
been converted to a troopship and her passenger space had been
subdivided into smaller cabins. She could carry fifteen thousand
troops at a time. The first- and second-class passenger saloons were
rebuilt as theatres for the troops. Dutch liners like the *Johan van
Oldenbarnevelt*, mentioned in an earlier chapter as the *JvO*, had
been converted in England as well. The *JvO* survived, but her sister
ship, the *Marnix van St. Aldegonde*, filled with troops, was torpedoed in the Mediterranean and sank. There were no casualties,
however; another Dutch liner in the same convoy, the *Ruijs*, came
to the rescue, stopped nearby and sent all her life boats across to the
Marnix, saving the entire crew and troops with herself still under
attack.

As mentioned, the fastest and most modern liner, the *Oranje*, became a hospital ship and was painted white with large red crosses. She was never attacked, either by U-boats or by aircraft; nor was the *Oranje* escorted by allied warships or aircraft. The *Queen Mary* was escorted by long-range aircraft while we were on board and, earlier in the war, by a cruiser. One escort cruiser was accidentally sliced into two by the *Queen Mary's* bow and sunk when it tried to cross the bow while the *Queen Mary* was going full speed. Many lives were lost in that horrible accident. With her strong bow and, more importantly, her twenty-eight-and-a-half knots speed, the *Queen Mary* was virtually unscathed.

Having very little "refugee" luggage, the four of us settled quickly and took a trip around the big vessel just as she was leaving port. We soon noticed that the majority of the passengers were American flight crews on their way back to the U.S. on leave, perhaps continuing on to the Pacific. There were also many Poles, Norwegians and Czechs and, of course, British, but we seemed to be the only Dutch and perhaps the youngest passengers. During the day, the passengers were allowed outside on the deck. Playing around with a primitive protractor and estimating the sun's declination, we figured out that the ship was initially well north of the great circle route, perhaps to be within range of an escort of aircraft based in Iceland.

At night, nobody was allowed on deck and portholes were covered. Day and night, nothing was allowed to be thrown overboard – cigarette cases, for example.

We were told that debris thrown from the ship might be picked up by a German submarine surfacing during the night, which could identify its source and pass this information on by radio to another sub further ahead, a remote possibility but still a reasonable precaution. The vessel zigzagged and was escorted by seaplanes taking turns but often out of sight when they were searching for U-boats ahead. As far as we knew, neither the *Queen Mary* nor her more modern sister, the *Queen Elizabeth*, were ever intercepted by the Germans.

Life on board was great. Not many passengers showed signs of sea sickness; the very large vessel was not all that lively, even in rough seas. The four of us junior passengers had a whale of a time playing poker, bridge or chess with the other passengers of a variety of nationalities. We found the Poles the most raucous guys, always arguing with each other about their card games. The American flight crews – and there were many – were very polite and seemed somewhat subdued, possibly because they were heading home after flying heavy bombers over Germany for several months. Quite a few women in the military service were among the passengers, but there were no dances or other social activities. Compared to the voyages of the other liners on which I served as a third or second mate in later years, the *Queen Mary's* passage was very uneventful. One afternoon, when we were all watching a movie in the large theatre, the *Queen Mary* had to make an emergency turn for whatever reason, resulting in a pile up of hundreds of men and women sliding with their chairs from one end to the other and then back again until the vessel returned to an even keel: a total chaos of bodies to be sorted out. No bones were broken.

The highlight of the voyage was our arrival in New York some four days after leaving Greenock. I kept thinking of brother Frits' reaction when, for the first time, he entered the harbour of New York as a junior mate in the early 1930s. The letter he wrote home went from house to house in our street. He "felt like entering a new world," I remember he wrote. I had a similar reaction but much stronger because life in my Holland was so much more difficult than in Frits' days.

The *Queen Mary* slowly and majestically passed the Statue of Liberty on her way to her berth in New York. We were welcomed by a fleet of decorated motor-cruisers, yachts and barges loaded with brass bands and chorus girls singing and dancing in patriotic costumes. We had not expected this show at all, but we realized that the noisy reception was meant for the returning U.S. airmen and not for just everyone on the *Queen Mary*. Even so, it was quite an introduction to the American lifestyle. The sight of New York's skyscrapers must have been an emotional experience for the thousands of American passengers on board – those who had survived the German anti-aircraft artillery and the Messerschmitts. I was overwhelmed as we closed in on the skyline, and so were my Dutch companions.

After our debarkation, a representative of the Ned Shipping (which, as mentioned earlier, was the semi-military administration of the Dutch merchant navy during the war) took us to the Times Square Hotel in the centre of New York. I was to report to the office of the Nederland Line in New York the next morning, and probably sail on the *M.S. Tarakan* to South America that same day. The three others were to stay in the hotel for a while to be assigned to another ship at a later date. When we entered the elevator, I ran into my KvdZ classmate, Biermans (1943/1944), who had joined the Ned Shipping fleet when the Canadians liberated Noord Brabant where he lived. Biermans was the big guy mentioned earlier in my KvdZ notes; he defended lightweights Bakker and Ages, sleeping near the dorm's entrance, against the midnight raiders from the dorm occupied by the two-year types – a silly age-old tradition of this anno 1780 institute.

The four of us were assigned two rooms high up in the Times Square Hotel (actually overlooking Times Square) – one room for the aspiring engineers and the other one for the aspiring navigators. Within minutes after unpacking our modest valises, the two engineers stormed into our room and told us that a couple of girls walked in and started to make friendly advances. These two guys had graduated from a very technical engineering school somewhere in the countryside where the emphasis was on engineering rather than on the temptations in foreign ports. An advantage of the KvdZ over other training schools surely was its location near the red light district of Amsterdam and our occasional communications with its inhabitants on Wednesday afternoons as well as the lectures of the KvdZ staff. My roommate and I went to our neighbours' room, said some nice and understanding things to the two ladies and suggested they go back to the lobby where they might pick up some guys with more money. They left with no hard feelings.

During our first walkabout in New York, we came across an obviously very American wartime ritual which I found a bit shocking. If, in a family, one or more members enlisted in the military services

and went overseas, the family would display a large blue star in their
window with the number of members involved. Casualties would
be represented by a gold star, again with a number. Commercial
buildings, shops and offices could display the same blue and/or gold
star for enlisted or fallen employees, apparently not just in New York,
but all over the U.S. I thought this type of "window dressing" was
uncalled for and would have been unacceptable in the Netherlands,
where school children have been looking after the graves of fallen
Canadians ever since the end of the war in 1945.

New York

After five years of blacked-out streets, houses and stores in
Holland, the brightly lit streets in New York looked almost unreal,
even though there seemed to be some sort of a "brown out" to dim
the lights in the higher levels of the sky scrapers. Dimming the
lights on the East Coast would make it more difficult for German
submarines operating at night to track ship silhouettes standing out
against the light of the coastal towns.

We were awe struck with the displays in the store windows, and
I kept thinking about my parents and friends with whom I'd have
liked to share my impressions. At a time difference of six hours, it
should have been early the next morning in Wassenaar. My father
and mother would just be getting up to face another cold and joyless
day; my father would rise first, to get the woodstove going, followed
by Mam when the living room was warm enough. What a change
in lifestyle for this previously so dynamic couple. After my introduction to the free world during the past couple of weeks, I slowly
started to become aware of the damage done to the millions in the
Netherlands by the ruthless Nazi fanatics and their servile follow-
ers. We could not even keep our dog. I was worried that my parents
might not live through the food shortage, even with my extra ration
card. There must have been thousands of elderly couples like them
in the big cities. Brother Nap did not concern me. He was a slick

and resourceful operator and he would outwit the Gestapo and the Grünen and certainly survive the hunger winter. But what about our neighbours Evert and Vera? Had they picked up my message from Radio Oranje in London on their short-wave radio frequency? When would I ever find out? I knew it had been transmitted from London exactly as scheduled because we received it on the short wave radio of the Hesselinks in Eindhoven as well. Just before leaving Eindhoven on March 10th, I wrote a letter to my parents and handed it to a member of the intelligence who had earlier interviewed me – a Dutchman. If and when the Germans surrendered, he expected to be among the first military to enter The Hague and would drive to Wassenaar to meet my parents (as I found out after the war, he did). My travel mates did not share my family concerns; they lived in the liberated southern part of the Netherlands.

All four of us had been brought up in or near what we thought were large cities in Western Europe, such as The Hague and Amsterdam. New York was not just another "big city;" it was New York! What struck me about New York was not so much the sight of skyscrapers or the Empire State Building, but the people, the New Yorkers. They seemed to be running around in all directions all the time like scared water bugs, never slowing down to have a look at some display in a shop window or an accident or a construction site. At a red stop light for a pedestrian crossing, they'd quickly open the morning paper to check the stock market, then fold it up just as fast when the light switched to green and start running again. Unlike Amsterdam, there were no canals with romantic little bridges and Amsterdammers leaning over the railing to watch and advise a guy trying to fish his lost hat out of the canal or some well-dressed Parisienne taking her equally well-dressed miniature poodle for a walk.

The New Yorkers spoke a funny sort of English, pronouncing a "th" as a "t" and an "i" as "oi." They were helpful. When asked for directions, they'd stop running and try to explain, but so quickly that when they had finished their rapid instructions, we were still trying to make sense of the first line. We did not have the courage to board a bus because we'd never be able to get off in time, but we did venture to enter the subway and managed to get out again. I found the subway much dirtier than the Underground in London, most likely because the tracks were closer to the surface, with the gratings part of the street pavement. During the voyage on the Queen Mary, we befriended a couple of American airmen who described to us the ethnic sections of New York and made us realize that our one-day excursion would only cover a small part of the city.

The Tarakan

The next day, around the fourth of April, I went to the office of the Nederland Line in New York and introduced myself to the boss, captain Arie Steen, a kind man with a secretary who spoke her own mixture of Dutch and English: "Ik ben zo zorry maar doe de door dicht" (I am so sorry but close the door) – a nice lady who looked after Captain Steen like a mother, telling him to fix his suspenders while talking to me. It was a very informal and pleasant office, quite different from Amsterdam. Captain Steen told me that brother Frits was doing fine, somewhere in the Pacific; they had already notified him about his kid brother's escape from occupied Holland. Obviously, communications between London and New York and the fleet out in the ocean were in good shape. After the usual paperwork, I signed on as an apprentice officer on the Tarakan departing from New York to Rio de Janeiro on April 6th.

My three travel mates stayed in New York for a couple of weeks and would then travel to San Francisco to board other vessels.

Captain Steen was the inspector of the sea-going deck personnel of the Nederland Line based temporarily in New York during the war. If I understood it rightly, fleets of the large shipping companies originally based in Amsterdam, like the Nederland Line, and Rotterdam, like the Holland America Line, were still administered by their original owners mainly in New York, but certain aspects such as time charters and insurance were looked after by the Netherlands Shipping Committee (the Neth Shipping).

This committee was established by the Dutch government in exile, along with providing my clothing. Neth (or Ned) Shipping apparently had financed our trips from Eindhoven to London and on the *Queen Mary* to New York, with generous contributions from women's committees in South America. I had absolutely nothing when I arrived in Eindhoven – not even money, which I had given to the guys who helped me carry the boat and who had needed some persuasion to accept it.

The *Tarakan* was one of the seven so-called T-boats of the Nederland Line built in 1930, a versatile and graceful class of ships. In fact, when the first T-boat appeared on the U.S. west coast in the early thirties, an American naval architect called her the Rolls Royce of the ocean, so said the chief officer of the *Tarakan*, who had served on her maiden trip as a junior officer. The T-boats were named after islands in the Indonesian archipelago; Tarakan is an island east of Borneo. Others were the *Tajandoen* and the *Tanimbar*, both torpedoed with a large loss of life. These T-boats were designed for freight (around ten and a half thousand tons of one thousand kilograms of "deadweight," mostly cargo), twenty passengers, and transport of *hadjis* (pilgrims from Java and Bali to Djeddah, the port of Mekka) and back. The *Tarakan* was also equipped with large "deep" tanks mid-ship for transport of palm oil. Finally, many former Dutch university and high school students remember their summer vacations on the *Tarakan* in the Norwegian fjords. The *Tarakan's* upper deck was covered with another deck of wooden planks, mainly to keep the underlying 'tween deck (where the *hadjis* slept) cool and to allow the *hadjis* to sleep and cook outside in tents during passage in the Indian Ocean, weather and wind permitting

During the war, the *Tarakan*, with a speed of fourteen and a half knots (one knot, or nautical mile per hour being equivalent to 1.85 kilometres per hour) and heavy armament, was considered an auxiliary cruiser and did not travel in convoy. En route to Rio de Janeiro, the *Tarakan* was not escorted by the navy or airforce. Her armament consisted of ten centimetre guns forward and aft in gun turrets, several twenty millimetre Oerlikons and Hotch Kiss anti-aircraft guns, depth charges against submarines and even a kite dragging a steel cable to deter enemy aircraft, and a degaussing cable against the magnetic mines triggered by the steel of a passing ship. The vessel was blacked out at night and we did not yet have the convenience of radar.

I was on the twelve to four watch with the chief officer, Mr. Manschot, and, having listened to the grim stories of my seasoned shipmates about some of their colleagues going down with their ships after a torpedo from a German sub, I couldn't help but keep a wary eye on the sea around us. And it happened: three torpedoes in formation heading straight for the bow. I gasped, paralysed by the sight of these sleek lethal monsters. I covered my face with one hand and held the railing with the other. Nothing happened. They were dolphins chasing our bow to play with. Fortunately, Mr. Manschot had not been looking at me.

Apart from the rendezvous with the crazy dolphins, the voyage to Rio was somewhat uneventful, although a great experience for me as a brand new apprentice. Before the war, apprentices with the Nederland Line, and surely with other shipping companies, had a tough time keeping focused on their aspiration to specialize in navigation and seamanship. According to brother Frits, who started his career as an apprentice with the Nederland Line in the early 30s, most of his time onboard went to such activities as washing the deck and sanding and varnishing the ship's railings. He and his fellow apprentices spent little time on learning how to drop a ship's anchor or to lower a life boat, or even how to use a sextant on a moving ship, skills they could not have picked up at school. When I boarded the *Tarakan*, I prepared myself for a similar life... but shared none of his complaints. Perhaps the new generation of officers and crew was more liberal minded and did not want to treat us the same way. From what I heard on ships in later years, Frits was one of those liberals. During the war, apprentices had become a rarity. The officers did not really know what to do with these kids. Then again, the new apprentices were products of the German oppression and the hunger winter. They were only too grateful to start a new life. My life as an apprentice throughout the (compulsory) year was a blast!

I had to get used to the rich meals onboard, and to my picky table companions. During my first dinner at the officers' table, one of the engineers sent his steak back to the galley because it wasn't cooked to his taste. A STEAK. I lost my cool and gave him a piece of my mind, to the embarrassment of the other people at the table. I left the table and walked around on deck for a while until the second mate, a friend of Frits, came up and we had a good talk about the starving Dutch trapped in Holland and the not-so-starved Dutch at sea, risking their lives to liberate their countrymen. Eventually we'd all get to know each other a bit better.

As a crew member on an auxiliary cruiser, I had to take part in gunnery practice and the Surinam gunners never seemed to tire of teaching the *leerling* (Dutch for apprentice) how to hit a floating target with an Oerlikon. Then there were practices with pistols and revolvers and in releasing anti-sub depth charges and kites dragging steel wires above the ship to harass dive-bombers (e.g., in the Mediterranean). However, I could not have a go at one of the two ten centimetre heavies fore and aft. Best of all the practices were star shots at dusk with the second mate on the four to eight watch. We did not see much of the coast, but crossed the impressive sediment-laden plume of the Amazon well out of sight of the coast.

Rio de Janeiro

At a speed of fourteen and a half knots, or twenty-seven kilometres an hour, with bunkering fuel in Trinidad, it took the *Tarakan* about four weeks to get from New York to Rio de Janeiro, just in time to help the Dutch community in Rio celebrate the liberation of Holland on May 5th. The Dutch ambassador had invited the entire crew of the *Tarakan* to the party. Our young English radio operator, Eric Wetherell, and I met two Dutch sisters, Gerri and Trudy, during the party and were invited by their parents, Mr. and Mrs. Jordan, to spend the night at their condo on Copacabana, overlooking the vast beach of Rio. So we did and had an early morning swim in the ocean while thinking of the celebration in Holland. It must have been a happy late afternoon in Holland while we were cavorting in the waves at Copacabana. We went to the top of the famous mountain Pâo de Assucar (Sugar loaf) and even watched a movie in Portuguese that I, of course, couldn't follow. The girls were fluent in three languages: Dutch, Portuguese and English. Eric, typically for an Englishman, made no effort to learn even the most elementary words in Portuguese.

When we left the theatre, we noticed a large neon sign on top of one of the highest buildings: "Il presidente Truman accaba de affirmer que Hitler esta realmente morte." I had long awaited the message that Hitler really was dead, but never expected it to be in Portuguese! It was worth memorizing.

The next day, Sunday, was supposed to be a day of reflection and meditation but turned out to be a bit of a shocker. The exultant Dutch decided to make it a day of thanks. Eric and I were still staying at the Jordan's and the four of us youngsters decided to go to church. After a spirited sermon by the minister (in Dutch), the very large congregation kneeled and prayed. Agnostic Eric and I remained standing in the back row while the girls kneeled and prayed. Two more people in the front row remained standing. One turned around – the captain, with the chief officer and two ladies. Captain Roeterink tapped the chief on his shoulder and pointed back to us. We had completely forgotten about the ship throughout these three days and hadn't notified anybody of our whereabouts. We nudged the girls and pointed at the "old man" (the captain) and the chief. All four of us managed to move back and quietly disappear into an anteroom to figure out what to do. However, the captain and chief were right behind us. The captain was furious. He reminded us that the *Tarakan* was to depart later on the same day and that he was about to contact the military police. I'd get no more shore leave. Eric got away with a reprimand because he was actually not with the Nederland Line but "on loan" or whatever from a British radio telegraph company. We kissed the girls a fond goodbye and had one of the locals row us back to the *Tarakan* anchored nearby. So ended my one and only visit to Rio de Janeiro, but not my faithful correspondence with Gerri for many years. We met later in Boston and New York.

São Paulo

We departed for Santos that same afternoon to take on (if I remember this well) a load of wheat, part of the relief supply for Holland. It takes less than one day to steam from Rio to Santos, the harbour of the very large industrial city of São Paulo. Apprentice Ages had to go back to chipping and painting just like the good old days before the war. The captain came up to check on my progress and found me sound asleep on one of the deck chairs. The worst punishment was that I had to stay on board while everyone else was sightseeing ashore. But not for very long. After we tied up in Santos, I noticed a well-dressed woman come up the gangway and knock on the door of the captain's room. Shortly after that, the captain called me in, introduced me to the lady and said, "Leerling, you are to go with Mrs. Fonkert, the head of the Brazilian Red Cross, who will interview you about your experiences in Holland during the German occupation. She will take you to her house in São Paulo."

I couldn't believe my ears. I took a shower and got dressed and went back to the captain, who was still talking to the lady in Dutch. Apparently, some Dutch people in Rio had advised her that a boy on the *Tarakan* had escaped from Holland before the liberation and could give her all the details about the hunger winter and what was needed most urgently in food and other relief supplies. The woman's husband, Dr. Fonkert, was also Dutch. He was the director of the textile consortium Matarazzo.

I do not remember all the details of my visit to São Paulo sixty years ago, but I vividly recall the remarkable skill with which Mrs. Fonkert navigated through the heavy traffic on the freeway while keeping up and animated conversation about Holland. I also still remember noticing, as we approached São Paulo from the coastal lowlands, an abrupt change in scenery into reddish plateaus of what looked like limestone, well above sea level. Sâo Paulo is about sixty kilometres inland from Santos – about half an hour's drive on the freeway; surely more like fifteen minutes for Mrs. Fonkert . . . .

The hacienda of the Fonkert family was well outside Sâo Paulo – a very attractive villa with an orchid plantation, Dr. Fonkert's private lifetime project. The couple had one son of my age, a neat guy who later drove me around to do some sightseeing. I don't remember his first name. Unlike his parents, he did not speak Dutch very well, but his English interlarded with Portuguese was about as good as mine without, so we had some good laughs. He revealed that he had heard all about me last afternoon in Rio when our captain had spotted the radio operator and me with the two Jordan sisters in the church after we had disappeared without a trace. The story went all around the Dutch community the following day. He said that we were lucky to escape arrest by the Brazilian police on a warrant while the *Tarakan* was about the leave.

After dinner, Mrs. Fonkert and I got together in her office to do some serious business. We had a lengthy and I'd say very productive session about Brazil's contribution to alleviating the desperate shortage of food, clothing and almost anything else needed to help the Dutch people to get back on their feet. We finished around midnight with a Brazilian nightcap. Mr. Fonkert's junior drove me back to the *Tarakan* the next morning to be taken on a guided tour of the ship before we left Santos.

I did not hear about my cancelled shore leave anymore. Mrs. Fonkert must have softened our captain. It would not take this attractive lady much to make the old seadog change his mind.

11

HOMEWARD BOUND

Shortly after my return from Sâo Paulo, the *Tarakan* cast off to
head back to New York. We passed Rio de Janeiro early the
next morning. I tried to find Copacabana through my binoculars,
but the beach was hidden behind some local hills. I couldn't help
thinking up some what-ifs about our bizarre last day in Rio – e.g.,
what if the old man hadn't looked back during the service or had not
gone to church at all? Brazil was at war with Germany and Eric and
I were in military service, so the military police would have located
us, let the girls go home and kept Eric and me to be booked, possibly
as AWOL (absent without leave), and hopefully sent us overland
to Santos to meet the *Tarakan*. We made a mistake, whether or
not generated by the VE day celebrations. I could just imagine Mr.
Jordan telling his daughters, "I told you, stay away from sailors!"

After another uneventful voyage along the coast of Brazil and
Florida, we returned to New York around the middle of June. The
Tarakan stayed in port for about a month to be made shipshape
for her much-anticipated return to Amsterdam after surviving five
years of hostilities and losing two of her sisters, the *Tanimbar* in an
air raid and the *Tajandoen* by torpedo.

When the ship was tied up, I lay down on my bunk for a little
snooze. Mient de Jong, our second mate, came in and handed me
a letter.

"From your brother."

Looking at the writing on the envelope, I immediately recognized
Frits' uniquely broad style of writing. It moved me to tears for the
first time since being picked up at night by a Canadian patrol after
I had crawled out of the water near the Moerdijk bridges. Mient de

Jong discreetly left me with the letter. I spent a lot of time reading every word and expression to figure out what made him tick, seven years after he'd left home. His style of writing had not changed and, judging by his comments, neither had my brother himself. We would not meet for several months, when Frits was sent to the then Dutch Indies to take charge of the Nederland Line harbour facilities in Tandjong Priok near Batavia (now Djakarta) and when I arrived there on the *Tarakan.*

Before sending his letter through the U.S. Fleet Post Office, Frits had already sent me a significant amount of money to go shopping in the U.S. for the family in Wassenaar. He assumed that I'd be in Holland before he would be and also had a better idea about what was needed. Moreover, my own salary had been upped with a bonus of one hundred dollars a month – "danger money" for anybody in the Dutch merchant navy, regardless of rank or service. One hundred dollars was, in those days, a large amount. Frits had always advised me to join the merchant navy and not the cheapskate navy, which provided no danger money, lousy food, strict discipline, poor accommodation, and not enough life boats. At any rate, with Frits' generous donation and my own income, the money factor did not limit my spending spree after my daily chores to prepare the ship for the voyage to Holland.

Based on my discussions with Mrs. Fonkert in Sâo Paulo, my purchases zeroed in on rice, coffee, tea, sugar, cooking oil, canned meat and fish, flour, spices, chocolate, and soap. And on those items not suggested by Mrs. Fonkert: cigarettes, cigars and tobacco, which were cheap in the U.S. and duty-free in our case; moreover, I had started to light up myself. I also bought bicycle tires – a gamble because of the size of Dutch cycles.

Then there was the girls' stuff: nylon stockings, lipstick, perfume. Some of the guys on board were reluctant to get involved with this type of merchandise and delegated me to do it.

All in all, it was an instructive job for a week or so and it improved my business English. I took some time off to stay with one of Frits' girlfriends living outside New York, Mary Gibson. She drove me around in the scenic Hudson Valley for a few days. It was my first time visiting a drive-in theatre (remember reader, this was 1945, not 1975).

A day before the *Tarakan* cast off, several crew members of other vessels embarked to make the trip back to Holland with us. They had been trapped like Frits in various parts of the world when the war broke out and had continued to serve with the allies. They went home as passengers to go on extended leave or retire.

Before heading for Holland, the *Tarakan* entered the Gulf of Mexico to take on more cargo in New Orleans and Houston. Captain Roeterink introduced me to a family, the Edmunds, in New Orleans with whom he had become acquainted during the war. Their twenty-year-old daughter, Ada, was a fanatic sharpshooter – a great sport. We spent much of the evening competing in shooting targets in their garden and, after my rifle lessons from the gunners on the *Tarakan*, I think I really surprised her. Her family invited me for dinner the next evening. However, when I walked to their house, some kid threw a wad of bubble gum on my hair from an upstairs window. I couldn't get it out and bought Aqua Velva, which dissolved it, but the stuff smeared all over my head after it had evaporated. I had to excuse myself to Mrs. Edmunds, went back to the ship and decided not to leave the *Tarakan* anymore until arriving in Amsterdam.

The Mississippi was a disappointment: a dirty, muddy, shallow channel bordered by swamps, sadly hanging willows and garbage.

After calling at New Orleans and Houston, the *Tarakan* did not return to New York but headed straight for Holland. We were in the Atlantic in beautiful weather on the sixth and ninth of August when we heard on the radio that Hiroshima and Nagasaki in Japan and been destroyed by two American atomic bombs. Preoccupied with our return to Holland, we paid little attention to this brief news item and it was not until much later that the reality of the disasters' consequences started to sink in.

Home

We arrived in Rotterdam on August 28th, 1945. Several of us living in southwest Holland disembarked here while the *Tarakan* unloaded; others went on to Amsterdam. A big open truck arrived in Rotterdam to pick us and our luggage up and, sitting on our spoils, we headed out to our various homes in the province. Singing at the top of our voices, we arrived in Wassenaar and unloaded apprentice Ages to his ecstatic parents, who had been advised by the Nederland Line of my imminent return. I'd had no contact with them since leaving, barring the radio message of my safe crossing intercepted and relayed by Evert. Crying "m'n jongen, m'n jongen!" (my boy, my boy), Mam almost fell on her face trying to climb on the fender to kiss me and all the other cheering guys on the truck. My father was a bit more composed. There were flags in the street to welcome young Ages home. I imagine Mam had made sure that everybody knew about my arrival. I handed out cigarettes and lipstick and all kinds of stuff to the neighbours and almost felt like a Canadian tank crew entering a liberated village. It was a great welcome, but the truck had to leave. The other men had to go home too, and they had been away so much longer.

My parents looked thin but otherwise mentally back to their normal sprightly attitude and full of "projects." To my surprise, they had decided to sell their house and, supported by the proceeds and their pension, move to my father's beloved Friesland – quite an undertaking at their age. They had already made plans to build a small house in a village near the southwest coast of the province, Oude Mirdum.

Except for the piano, the living room was back to normal with the enormous Philips radio in place. I remembered the many uncomfortable evenings I had spent in the wainscot under the roof listening with my headphones to the BBC or Radio Oranje until the electricity had been cut off. The acute shortage of food during the hunger winter had been remedied by air droppings and ships.

I went to our neighbours, Evert and Vera, to thank them for their efforts to pick up the message of the rhinoceros on the London-based

Radio Oranje. On my way to their house, I walked past the grave of our Great Dane Sobat Juul and stood still for a while, choked up. Evert and Vera were home and told me all about the Saturday evening when Evert had put on his earphones and picked up the message right on schedule. The message had been "De Rhinoceros is door het oog van de naald gekropen" (The Rhinoceros has crawled through the eye of the needle). Brother Nap had also received the message on his short-wave receiver and told me later that it was a stupid, typically juvenile joke and that he wasn't the least bit surprised at my mother's reaction. Maybe so, but I just wanted to somewhat break with the standard, rather boring communications within the Resistance. I visited Johan and some friends and found everybody still talking about the joyous entry of the Canadians in May. It was nice to see Stien again, in great spirits, and her father and his rich potato patch. People were so grateful to have survived the hunger winter even though so much was still needed to restore their normal lives.

I joined the *Tarakan* again a couple of days later to help out on the bridge when a skeleton crew took her from Rotterdam to the home port, Amsterdam. There was destruction all around, but I don't remember any problem in the locks at IJmuiden. The harbour of Amsterdam was a mess of fallen cranes and big holes in the quays. This unnecessary destruction had obviously been carried out by a frustrated and vindictive German navy commander. Such an act was not professional, certainly not "scorched earth" because the war was over.

A couple of days after our arrival in Amsterdam, Nap and Welmoet visited while I was on watch. They went into the galley and found a garbage can half filled with cooked rice under the counter. They scooped it all into a bag and took it home. The hunger winter was not over yet . . . .

Some Final Reflections

"How in the hell did you get away with it?" asked a member of the British Intelligence who interviewed me in Zevenbergse Hoek. The Canadian patrol had taken me there to have a nap and dry out in front of the fireplace. I had indeed been very fortunate that night, capsizing near the shore instead of midstream, clearing a booby trap, walking over or past landmines in the frozen ground left behind by the retreating Germans, and being picked up by a Canadian patrol alerted by the explosion of the booby trap – all in the middle of the night.

The intelligence guy called in two members of the Dutch Resistance to check the authenticity of my Parool ID and other documents, still moist from the dunking. They seemed to be regular couriers who had made their crossing in the evening further east and then by car through liberated territory to deliver some films. They had actually watched my crossing in broad daylight and called me an idiot to pull it off right under the eyes of a German guard who, for some reason of his own, did not shoot me in the back as I paddled away. Apparently, a girl courier further upstream had been shot trying to do the same thing. The Englishman had a better sense of humour and had some good words for the local people advising me on the route past the German positions. He even asked me if I'd be interested in trying another trip. I declined.

"When you paddled past the breakwater at Sliedrecht and you suddenly faced an armed German guard, what went through your mind?" I was once asked. "Were you scared of being shot and did you think of people at home?"

These are images we sometimes read about in a novel but, having just turned twenty, I was still a single-minded young kid whose thoughts had reached a state where nothing mattered other than crossing the river. If I had seen the German take his gun off his shoulder, I might have surrendered, but I doubt it. There was no turning back.

Looking back at all the lucky breaks I had during the crossing and at such episodes as reclaiming my bike "requisitioned" by the

Germans, slipping through *razzias* (including the one by a member of the Luftwaffe who didn't like that sort of recruitment and let me go), avoiding arrest by the Brazilian military police in Rio de Janeiro in the nick of time thanks to the captain of the *Tarakan*, and, most of all, escaping a V2 by just the width of one street while having lunch in London, 1945 seemed to be my year of grace.

Eight years later, my Dutch friend Jan ter Hart, also a former mate with the Nederland Line, sponsored my emigration to Canada. He became my patient and forgiving teacher in the land survey of Saskatchewan until I went back to the ocean to survey the coastal waters in British Columbia and the Arctic and work on the prevention of oil spills. Having followed my capers during the war, Jan's wife Sophia suggested that I had been protected by my Guardian Angel – thus the title of these memoirs.

But it wasn't just a Guardian Angel who had guided me to freedom. There were some sympathetic countrymen, total strangers who advised me on the route to take and even helped carry the kano through the war zone; and a couple of German guards who should have stopped and arrested me but didn't, possibly because they were the older types who were most likely disenchanted with the state of affairs in their country. As for the younger generation among the Germans, an incident comes to mind when Sobat Juul was still with us. I took her for a walk in the dunes. Angered that the Germans had no right to use our dunes for their military operations and structures, I took her right through a gate marked "Sperrgebiet" (restricted area). A young German soldier came dashing down the dune to stop us.

"Halt! Sonst wirst du erschossen!" (Halt or else you'll be shot).

"Wir sind keine Spione, Ich wollte mal mit meinem Hund spazieren gehen!" I yelled back and kept walking (We are no spies. I just want to take my dog for a walk.").

He ran over and physically blocked my passage, but seemed more embarrassed than angry. He did not take his rifle off his shoulder to threaten me and I had to give him credit for that. We stood there facing each other for a few moments, then I said, "Kom, Sobat." She had patiently followed the confrontation.

"Danke," the German said, obviously relieved.

He didn't have to thank me for walking away. After all, he was in charge, cum fraude or not. He remained courteous and, behind his hated Nazi uniform, he was probably a good man. The incident stuck in my mind for a long time and I started to concur with my parents' attitude of not judging a person by his uniform or even by a logo like a swastika. But how did a group of goons and some submissive intellectuals in Germany manage to dominate the entire country and raise hell in much of the world in such a short time? Will we be in for another, much more lethal disaster?

On the tenth of September, 1944 I watched one of the first V2s rise above the woods in Wassenaar and turn west to England. It was only the beginning of hundreds more launches during the following months. As I happened to witness the landing of a V2 in London and listened to the howl of approaching ambulances, I couldn't help visualizing a future confrontation with even more destructive weapons. They might already have been designed secretly somewhere by unscrupulous scientists or engineers. I only hope that we learned our lesson from the waste and devastation of WWII and that memoirs such as this may act as a convincing cautionary tale for future generations. If they fail to do so, then we have not learned anything.

ACKNOWLEDGEMENTS

After an impromptu school talk about the war years in Holland and a teacher's suggestion to put my stories in writing, I decided to give it a try, in particular when my friends at the Institute of Ocean Sciences offered to help with the manuscript. Jessica Hutchings, who processed data for Jim Gower, head of Remote Sensing at the institute, was aware of my reluctance to use a computer and volunteered many evenings and weekends over a two-year period to type and review the manuscript. Without her—and Jim's—persistent encouragement I might have lost interest in this lengthy project. Similarly, I am grateful to Diane Masson, who selected the illustrations and helped to organize the text, and to Lynne Armstrong for her skill in creating the book's cover and drawing the sketches and maps.

Thanks are due to Nadya Steiner for her corrections of my flawed German expressions, as well as to Jim and Ann Gower for drawing my attention to occasional slips of the Queen's English.

Finally, a word of gratitude to my son, Erik, who volunteered much of his busy workload as a graphic designer to compile a considerable amount of information into a manageable series of episodes in the book.

ABOUT THE AUTHOR

A lard Ages was born in Soestdijk, the Netherlands, in 1924 and was raised in Wassenaar near the coastal city of The Hague. After graduating from the gymnasium in Leiden and the *Kweekschool v.d. Zeevaart* (nautical college) in Amsterdam, Al left German-occupied Holland as a courier of the Resistance and enlisted in the Dutch merchant navy as an apprentice. He returned to liberated Holland in the late summer of 1945, and continued his seafaring life through the ranks of the third and second mate in the Nederland Line until he emigrated to Canada in 1953.

After working as a chainman in Saskatchewan, Al returned to sea to survey the coastal waters of B.C. and the Arctic during the summers, while attending U.B.C. in the winters. He obtained a Master's degree in fluid dynamics. His thesis analyzes the use of rising air bubbles to alleviate river sedimentation.

As an hydraulic engineer with the Government of Canada's Tides and Currents Group under Syd Wigen, Al worked on the development and verification of the first numerical models of harbours and estuaries and became involved in the prevention and containment of marine oilspills. He retired in 1991, but continues his work with the Institute of Ocean Sciences as a research engineer emeritus in Victoria, British Columbia, Canada.

ISBN 142511804-6

9 781425 118044